Additional Student Quotes

(Continued from back cover)

"The book provides the opportunity to get to know the men behind their political actions, and reveals the personal histories that lay the foundation for the men's future roles as the leaders of the United States of America."

— **Valerie Chen,** 9th grade

"It was interesting to see how some seemingly 'average' men have gone on to become some of the most famous in history. It gives me hope to achieve some greatness too."

— **Lauren Claravall,** 12th grade

"Gives hope to all students who think just because they didn't do great at all school subjects, they can still do great things in life."

— **Christina Dwyer,** 9th grade

"It is good to be reassured the presidents aren't always perfect."

— **Courtney Coker,** 9th grade

"I've never even heard of this president (James Polk), and yet it is so fascinating, a sickly boy becoming the greatest one-term president"

— **Henry Ma,** 7th grade

"It was very interesting and entertaining. The words paint a picture making the president's life easy to understand. It was very informative and much more interesting than a history book."

— **Kristen Nguyen,** 9th grade

"It was very interesting to read, because these presidents went through the same phases that I am going through as a teenager. This challenged me to reflect on myself. Mr. Wasserman has ignited a small flame and passion for reading that is to grow even stronger."

— **Susan Choi,** 11th grade

 www.trafford.com

North America & international
toll-free: 1 888 232 4444 (USA & Canada)
fax: 812 355 4082

PRESIDENTS WERE TEENAGERS TOO

Dedicated To My Grandchildren

Jerett Stephen Wasserman
Raishel Dion Wasserman
Taylor Leigh Wasserman
Logan Ross Wasserman
Justine Lynn Wasserman
Landyn Elizabeth Wasserman
Jonah David Wasserman
Mason Jake Wasserman
Julianne Emme-Roze Wasserman

Table of Contents

FOREWORD

My brother Sandy is three years older than I am, and he was my first mentor and then my life-long friend. Sandy looked out for his little brother – always involving me with his group of friends – and I looked up to him. When Sandy got his drivers license, we set out together on great adventures. We drove to Michigan's Upper Peninsula to fish, and later drove out West and down to Mexico.

At that time in our lives, we had no inkling that we would later serve together in Congress. And that's a lesson I've learned many times: you never know what life has in store for you.

Presidents Were Teenagers Too is a wonderful book because it gives readers a glimpse of what some of the greatest leaders in our nation's history were like when they were young. Readers will find in these pages that many Presidents did not know where their lives were heading either. Most of the Presidents' families "knew" their son would go on to greatness, but a few thought their son would never amount to much!

In my own life, one of my greatest disappointments became my greatest opportunity. I had applied for a Fulbright Scholarship to study and work abroad, but I wasn't selected. It was a real disappointment, but it turned out to be a lucky break. Soon, something better for me came along: the chance to run for the U.S. Senate.

Of course, I was only able to seize the opportunity because of what had happened in my life until that point. Sandy and I were fortunate to be part of a family that valued public service. Growing up during the Franklin Roosevelt and Harry Truman Administrations, the nightly conversations at our dinner table were about politics and current events. It was an exciting time, and we discussed how the United States could win World War II and then win the peace once the fighting stopped. Our parents inspired us to be active first in school and then in our communities.

Readers of this book will discover how mostly hard work and some amount of good fortune led 42 Americans to public service and, ultimately, the presidency. I hope that these fascinating stories will inspire readers to find in their hearts their own bright dreams and to never stop striving to reach them. You never know what opportunities life may have in store for you.

Senator Carl Levin

July 2006

Carl Levin is the senior U.S. Senator from Michigan. His brother, Sander Levin, represents Michigan's 12th District in the House of Representatives.

ACKNOWLEDGEMENTS

This book could not have been written had it not been for the research done by so many authors of previous biographies, all of whom are listed under References Used as Source Material at the end of this book.

I wish to thank Bill Raabe, an English and AP History teacher at Whitney High School in Cerritos, California for allowing me to have his students review and critique the manuscript prior to being sent to the publisher. Their comments were perceptive and helpful.

I wish to thank Hesh Cohen and Joan Flax for taking their precious time, as parents, to review and recommend needed corrections. They were very supportive of my project.

I wish to thank my instructor, Kaye Klem, who teaches a writing class at the Senior Center in Cypress, California. Kaye and members of the class all contributed with extremely helpful comments and suggestions as I read a chapter to them each week.

I wish to thank Aaron Ricchio, a senior at the time at Los Alamitos High School, for his imagination for the front cover design of this book.

I wish to thank my sister Regina (Jeannie) Spiszman for the many times she has proofread the manuscript since its inception.

I wish to thank Amy Lakin for devoting herself to the copy editing of this book. Her insight proved invaluable.

Last, but not least, this book would never have been written had it not been for the encouragement of my wife, Fernie, and my three sons, Michael, Craig and Marc.

A special thanks to my former high school friend, Carl Levin, for encouraging me to read when I wasn't inclined to do so.

Although my research found inconsistencies and contradictions, this in no way affected the message I wanted from this book --- to inspire and motivate as many people as possible – especially teenagers.

Preface To Revised Edition

Not in my lifetime .

There are events that you wish for, and realize that for whatever reason those events won't happen in your lifetime.

In 1955 there were many people who thought putting a man on the moon would never happen in their lifetime.

The same was true in 1961 when John F. Kennedy, a Catholic, ran for the presidency of the United States and won.

Now in 2008, 143 years since the days of slavery in our county, we have an African-American, Barack Obama, in the White House.

I have been very fortunate to see many things in my lifetime that were thought to be only science fiction.

It gives me hope that everything is possible in the United States of America.

The key, in my opinion, to having a better and safer world is to have everyone obtain a liberal education.

Benny Wasserman
2008

Preface To 2nd Edition

I feel fortunate to have written a book about U.S. presidents which included our first African American president - Barack Hussein Obama.

Now, I have lived long enough to see a president, Donald J. Trump, who has never held a public office, nor was a military leader, as were many former American presidents of our country.

Dwight Eisenhower, our 34th president was our last president who never held public office, but was one of our military heroes during World War II.

Our U.S. Constitution says that the only qualifications for the presidency of the United States of America is to be born a citizen in the U.S., be at least 35 years old, and to have never been convicted of a felony. There are no other requirements. This allows all U.S. citizens from all kinds of backgrounds to run for political office.

I hope this would inspire citizens of all ages to participate in running our government at all levels.

This is why the words of Abraham Lincoln during his Gettysburg address are so important:

"This is a country of the people, by the people and for the people."

Benny Wasserman
2016

NOTE TO THE READER

A few years ago an interesting question crossed my mind. Is there a book out there that tells about the teenage years of all the Presidents of the United States? Not only isn't there such a book, but these years are barely touched upon in most biographies of these respected leaders. I thought it would be interesting to find out how diverse their teenage years were, and how we might use this information to help inspire and motivate teenagers today – showing them that former presidents weren't necessarily much different than them.

There has been endless debate about whether leaders are born or made. What was it in our former presidents' makeup, in their temperaments or their personalities that pushed them forward and upward? Was it just luck at being in the right place at the right time? Why, in so many instances when presidents came from larger families, didn't others in the family rise to such heights? I believe not one president knew when he was a teenager that he would someday occupy the highest political office in the United States.

It is because of my strong belief that the teenage years are so pivotal in one's life that I thought I would write a book that focuses on the early years of the Presidents of the United States. When I first started my research, I believed I would find a common attribute in all forty-three presidents. That attribute, I thought, might be a love of reading. But after reviewing many biographies and autobiographies, I could not come to such a conclusion. What I can say is that *most* presidents did have a love of learning, and *many* were very talented speakers and good at debating.

There is no special training to become president. One must simply be thirty-five-years-old, a U.S. citizen, and not a convicted felon. It is true that in our inglorious past our U.S. Constitution didn't allow blacks (until the 15th Amendment in 1870 and then the Voting Rights Act of 1965) or women (until the 19th Amendment in 1920) to participate in our political democracy. Although no one from either group has yet become chief executive, each has made significant inroads into our political system. I am quite certain that we will see an African-American or a female president in the not so distant future.

By sharing our former presidents' shortcomings and weaknesses when they were most vulnerable and naive, in addition to their strengths and successes, we allow our youth to realize it is normal and part of growing up. Why should any person be stigmatized for the rest of his life because he committed indiscretions when he was a teenager?

The purpose of this book is to encourage adolescents to never give up. No one ever really knows his or her ultimate capability, and none of us has any idea what our limits truly are. Only by trying, and then trying harder, will we be able to see how much we can accomplish with our minds and bodies. The younger a person is when he recognizes that he has no mental limitations, the sooner he can rise to his full potential.

Few people go through life without experiencing some obstacles. When Herbert Hoover was unable to find work as an engineer after he graduated from college, he took a $2.00-a-day job as a gold miner's helper. Woodrow Wilson spent more than a year recuperating after he dropped out of college because of illness. George W. Bush did not get into law school, so he attended business school instead. All of the American presidents were motivated to move ahead in life, and were encouraged to persist, despite the roadblocks.

Some of our presidents, like George Washington and Calvin Coolidge, came from prosperous families. Others, like Abraham Lincoln and Bill Clinton, had little money for education or anything else. Yet these men were encouraged by their parents and teachers to learn and try new things, and they were driven to succeed. They all tried to get as much as they could from the world around them; they tried to understand and be a part of the world in which they lived.

There were those, such as Dwight Eisenhower and Gerald Ford, who were athletically inclined and could have gone on to play professional football. Thomas Jefferson and Harry Truman were both accomplished musicians. Theodore Roosevelt was a boxer who almost won the lightweight boxing championship. Each of America's presidents had a unique experience growing up, and each went on to become the most powerful man in the nation.

I encourage you the reader to draw your own conclusions about the early years of these men. Do you see a common trait that may have contributed to them becoming Presidents of the United States? Is there something in their personalities, their interests, or their upbringing that led them to become leaders? How often can you identify with our presidents? Perhaps someday I'll be adding a chapter about your teenage years...

ENJOY!

GEORGE WASHINGTON

First President of the United States
Lived: 1732 – 1799   Served: 1789 – 1797

George Washington, our nation's first president, spent most of his teenage years living with his half-brother who was fourteen years older. They had the same father but different mothers. Before George was born, his father had five children with his first wife. George was the first of five more children born in his father's second marriage. George's father, Augustine, who came from a fairly wealthy background, died when George was only eleven-years-old.

George Washington was born at Pope's Creek in Westmoreland, Virginia. His mother, Mary Ball, lived to be eighty-one-years-old, and she learned he was to be the first President of the United States just before she died.

George's father had sent his older sons to England to get the best education possible, but when he died, George's mother felt that she needed her children around her. Instead of giving George the same educational opportunities his half-brothers had, his mother sent him to inferior schools in the area. He also may have had some private tutoring from their indentured servants. George made a real effort to be a dutiful and helpful son, but from his teen years on, relations with his mother were strained. Although her husband left her with considerable money and land, Mary felt very much alone and insecure, and she became quite stingy. It is said that she was not only a selfish and possessive person, but that she could hardly read and write. There are few stories from George's youth that describe warm and happy events between mother and son.

1

There appear to be no records of George's teachers. In the few years that he did have some formal education, he liked arithmetic best. George probably learned more from his older half-brothers than he did from school. He never learned to write or spell very well, he read very little, and he was sorry about that all his life. By the time he was fourteen George could keep business accounts, write clear letters and do simple figuring, but he always felt he could have done more for the country if he had more schooling.

As George grew older, he loved vaulting, running and jumping, and no one rode horses better than he did. He was also an expert dancer and thoroughly enjoyed playing billiards. He had a number of boyhood romances and he liked to write love poems.

Growing up on a farm, George helped manage a plantation worked by twenty Negro slaves. He was observant and hardworking, and he saw all the things a plantation needed to operate, such as cloth and iron tools. He learned how to plant and produce tobacco, fruit, grains and vegetables.

It was also during his teenage years that George copied rules of behavior in an exercise book. He was very conscious of how he conducted himself in public. Following are some of his rules, with his original spelling and capitalization:

     1) Tis better to be alone than in bad company
     2) Use no Reproachful Language against any one
     3) Neither Curse nor Revile
     4) Be not Curious to Know the Affairs of Others
     5) Be careful to keep your Promise

When George was fifteen-years-old, he was already six feet tall and very strong. He was not afraid to fight other boys when the occasion arose, and he was never afraid to tell the truth. His only problem was that he got angry too easily. Instead of fighting, he turned to playing billiards and cards, and especially enjoyed the ritual of the foxhunt.

After hearing war stories from his older brother, George dreamed of becoming a sailor in the British Royal Navy. When he was fourteen, he decided he would go to sea. He would begin as a common sailor, and perhaps he could one day become captain of a ship. His brother thought it was a good idea, and helped him with his plans.

The day George was to board the ship, his mother received a letter from her brother telling her to stop George from enlisting in the navy. Her brother wrote that going out to sea was a nightmare for boys, that they were treated horribly. George was furious, but he had been taught to obey. A dutiful son, George did whatever his mother wanted him to do. She asked her brother for advice, and he suggested that rather than let George become a sailor, it would be better to apprentice him to a *tinker,* a mender of pots and pans.

After George gave up hope of becoming a sailor, he became interested in exploring the frontier. Becoming a surveyor and marking out new farms in the wilderness would give him a chance to leave home and seek adventure, and his mathematical mind enabled him to easily learn fractions and geometry. So he took his father's old set of surveying instruments out of storage and began to earn money as an assistant to local surveyors.

At the age of sixteen George gave up school completely and became a surveyor full time. He traveled around measuring land so people knew how much land they owned and exactly where the lines ran on their property. It was an occupation much in demand in colonial Virginia, where men's fortunes were counted in acres of tobacco rather than pounds of gold.

George was fortunate to be invited to go on a surveying expedition with Lord Fairfax, the largest property owner in Virginia. The month-long expedition set out on horseback in March 1748. George learned to sleep out in the open and hunt for food, and he was finally able to break away from his mother. By the time he returned home, he felt he had grown into a man. By the age of seventeen George was a professional surveyor, living away from home and supporting himself. His surveying work paid well. It was one of the few occupations in which a man could be paid in cash; most other businesses in Virginia were carried out with payment in tobacco.

When George was nineteen, Lawrence, his older brother who had tuberculosis, asked George to go with him to the Barbados Islands, because he thought he could get well there. It was the only time in his life that George was out of the country, and he contracted smallpox while he was there. After being sent home, he received news that Lawrence had died. This put an even greater burden on George, whose mother wanted more than ever to keep him at home.

While many encouraged George to go to college, his mother forbade him to leave home. She was afraid to be left alone with the estate left to her by her late husband. She lacked the passionate commitment to education that marked many other presidential mothers. George was the first of six presidents never to attend college.

At age twenty, without any training or experience in the military, George applied to the governor for a commission in the militia. Within a few months he was commissioned as a major and put in charge of training militia in southern Virginia. He immediately began reading books on tactics and military affairs, and two years later he was promoted to lieutenant colonel.

In 1752, at age twenty, Washington fell in love with a sixteen-year-old girl named Betsy. He proposed to her twice, but she refused to marry him. George fell in love many times before age twenty-seven, when he married Martha Dandridge Custis.

George Washington participated in the French and Indian War between the ages of twenty-two and thirty-one, and by the end of the war he had become a regimental commander. At age twenty-seven, while still a colonel in the army, Washington was elected to the House of Burgesses, where he remained a member until 1774.

The following year he became the commander-in-chief of the Continental Army, and he led during the American Revolution. He went on to become the first president of the thirteen colonies. George Washington was the only president elected by a unanimous electoral vote.

More Information About George Washington	
State Represented	Virginia
Party Affiliation	Federalist
School(s) Attended	Studied at home
Siblings	Sixth of Ten Children
Occupation(s)	Farmer/Planter, Surveyor, Soldier
Pet(s)	Horse named Nelson
Hobbies	Horseback Riding, Dancing, Billiards, Card Playing
States in Union During Teenage Years	Zero (Thirteen Colonies)

JOHN ADAMS

Second President of the United States
Lived: 1735 – 1826   Served: 1797 – 1801

John Adams was only five feet, six inches tall and very stocky. He was overwhelmed with illnesses throughout his ninety years. By the time he became president his hands shook with palsy and most of his teeth had fallen out due to gum disease. He refused to wear ill-fitting dentures and spoke with a lisp.

John, the eldest of three sons, was born in Braintree, Massachusetts. His father was a farmer, a deacon and a militia officer. His mother came from a leading family of merchants and physicians.

In his youth John preferred farm chores over schoolwork and books. While he was still a kid, Adams helped chop wood, clear away snow, look after the horses and cows, and work in the fields. He was not only a hard worker, but he also played hard. In the winter there was skating and sleighing, and in the summer there was fishing and swimming. He made toy boats and sailed them on local ponds and brooks. He flew kites, shot marbles and wrestled. John's favorite pastime was hunting. He spent every spare moment tramping through the woods after deer, partridge, grouse, squirrels and any other animal he could find. He even began to carry his gun to school so he could take it to the field without having to go home first.

In school he enjoyed studying agriculture which remained his hobby for life. He had an educated model in his uncle, a Harvard graduate who had been a schoolmaster and then a clergyman of some stature. John went to school in a little schoolhouse near his home, but he always wanted to play rather than study.

Having tried repeatedly and unsuccessfully to interest John in books, his father asked him if he would rather go to college or work, and what work he would like to do.

"I think I would rather try farming," said young John
Adams.

"Very well," said his father, "you may go to work in
the fields."

Young Adams went to work the very next day, working from sunrise to sunset. It was hard work, and it didn't leave the time for play that John was used to. He came home at night hungry, thirsty, tired, dusty, and stiff as a log.

"I think I would rather go to work among the books,"
he said, with his eyes on the ground, for he was
ashamed to look his father in the face.

"Very well," said his father, "This is what I want you
to do; go to college and get an education."

Having been taught to read by his father while still a young boy, Adams had a leg up on the other students in Mrs. Belcher's one-room schoolhouse. After digesting *The New England Primer*, he progressed to Joe Cleverly's Latin School. Adams hated his teacher there as much as he disliked the dreary assignments he was given. He clearly had an aptitude for math, and resented his teacher for not letting him progress at a faster rate. Disgusted, he worked through the math problems on his own at home. Except for math, he had little use for school and especially disliked Latin.

John's father had his heart set on his son attending Harvard College and becoming a minister, so John agreed to take his lessons more seriously if his father would get him out of Cleverly's school and into the more challenging classes of Joseph Marsh. During his year of study under Marsh, John at last began to earnestly explore the world of knowledge.

In 1751, at age sixteen, John entered Harvard College. Of all the classes he took, he most enjoyed math and philosophy. Adams joined a club in which members took turns reading aloud new publications, poetry and plays. The recitation demanded a certain theatrical flair, and the enthusiastic applause Adams received for his hearty renditions started him thinking about a career as a trial lawyer. His four years at Harvard turned him around intellectually: "I soon perceived a growing curiosity, a love of books, and a fondness of study which dissipated all my inclinations for sports."

John graduated from Harvard at the age of twenty, ranked fourteenth in a class of twenty-four. In those days a student's rank indicated social position, not scholarship, even though Adams was one of the best scholars in his class.

At age twenty-three, John was admitted to the bar as an attorney.

John Adams married Abigail Smith at age twenty-nine. They had four children — their oldest son became the sixth President of the United States, and two others died of alcoholism.

After a notable career as an attorney, Adams became a member of the Massachusetts legislature, a member of the Continental Congress, Ambassador to the Netherlands and Great Britain, and the nation's first Vice President, prior to becoming the second President of the United States.

More Information About John Adams

State Represented	Massachusetts
Party Affiliation	Federalist
School(s) Attended	Harvard College
Siblings	First of Three Children
Occupation(s)	Lawyer
Pet(s)	Horse named Cleopatra
Hobbies	Hunting, Reading, Fishing
States in Union During Teenage Years	Zero

THOMAS JEFFERSON

Third President of the United States
Lived: 1743 – 1826   Served: 1801 – 1809

Thomas Jefferson began to read when he was five-years-old, and he kept at it throughout his life. He had an insatiable curiosity about all aspects of life. Despite his many years in politics he never acquired two attributes usually considered essential to success in that profession: a thick skin and a gift for oratory.

Jefferson was born in Shadwell, Virginia. His father worked as a planter, surveyor and landowner. There is very little known about his mother other than the fact that she came from wealthy parents. She gave birth to ten children – Thomas was the third child and her first son.

Thomas was sent to boarding school when he was nine-years-old, where he was encouraged to read and write as frequently as possible. Tom spent almost nine months a year for the next five years at school, learning Latin, Greek and advanced mathematics. One of Tom's favorite subjects was philosophy, which today is known as science.

Tom's favorite teacher was the music master, who came six times a year. One day the music master invited Tom inside the drawing room and showed him a violin. When the master drew the bow over the strings, Tom instantly felt at peace. Tom learned to play the violin, and kept it up all through college.

Tom's father made sure his son had no chance to lose his edge. He kept him exercising and learning all summer in the fresh air. When his father could take time from surveying, he taught his profession to his son. His father also taught Tom how to shoot a gun, which he practiced for hours, until he was sure of his skill.

Tom was fourteen-years-old when his father died. Although his father was a wealthy farmer, he never had any schooling himself — but he wanted more for his children. So when he was gone, he left orders for four friends to advise Tom and continue his education until he reached the age of twenty-one.

As a youngster, Jefferson was interested in many subjects, and he kept careful records of everything that caught his attention. He wrote down the names of all the birds he saw in the area. Hunting was one of Tom's favorite pastimes, and he kept an exact record of every animal he shot. He listed its weight, size, color and any other fact he considered worthwhile. It was typical of young Jefferson to pay close attention to detail, and this was a practice that stayed with him throughout his life.

One thing Jefferson's friends could never understand about him — he loved studying. Many years later his friend James Maury said, "Even when we had an unexpected holiday from school, Tom always prepared the next day's lesson first and then went out to have fun."

Virginia had no public libraries at that time. Schoolmasters relied on the few books they had bought when they were in school, and hoped that a plantation owner would share books from his own private library. Most books had to be shipped from England. Generally, Tom and the other students made their own books by writing down rules for spelling and mathematics in their notebooks.

Because speaking in front of others was torture for Tom, the schoolmaster always made him recite aloud. No matter how much his teacher forced him, he was never comfortable speaking in front of large groups. Even at his inauguration as president he spoke in a whisper.

When Tom was sixteen, he decided to go to William and Mary College. Most of the boys played cards, raced horses, kept slaves and spent their money on fine clothes. Tom had fun, but his studies always came first. For fun he played the violin, danced with girls, and often went horseback riding. There was also good swimming nearby.

Whether riding his horse, studying nature or French or math, Jefferson did it wholeheartedly. Tom spent three to four hours a day practicing his violin. Despite all that, he found time to be with friends, attend an occasional party, and take part in a string quartet.

Tom filled every minute of every day with activity — he was never bored.

Tom was in his second year of college when he developed patterns of work and study that he would follow for the rest of his life. He awoke every morning at dawn to begin studying. The day was divided into class hours, meals, study, exercise, and more study before going to sleep at two o'clock in the morning.

Tom finished college and decided to become a lawyer. In those days it was possible for a man to become a lawyer in six weeks, but Tom felt it was important for a good lawyer to know other things in addition to law. So Tom studied history and science and geography. He learned to read and write in six languages. He got up every morning at five o'clock (to wake himself up he put his feet in cold water), and at night he studied long past midnight. He worked as an apprentice for five years, and then he became a lawyer at the age of twenty-four. He was never considered a first rate speaker, but he gained everyone's respect for his clear and brilliant writing on legal and government matters.

Soon after becoming an attorney he became a member of the House of Burgesses, and a member of the Virginia House of Delegates. He then served as Governor of Virginia, as a member of the Continental Congress, Minister to France, Secretary of State, and Vice President, prior to becoming the third President of the United States.

Thomas Jefferson fought for his country, but he did not fight with a gun or sword. He fought with words. He wrote one of the most famous papers in the world, and now the *Declaration of Independence* is known as one of the greatest papers in American history.

More Information About Thomas Jefferson	
State Represented	Virginia
Party Affiliation	Democratic-Republican
School(s) Attended	College of William and Mary
Siblings	Third of Ten Children
Occupation(s)	Lawyer
Pet(s)	Mockingbirds
Hobbies	Hunting, Playing Violin, Reading
Political Particulars	Drafted Declaration of Independence; Purchased Louisiana Territory
States in Union During Teenage Years	Zero

JAMES MADISON

Fourth President of the United States
Lived: 1751 – 1836   Served: 1809 – 1817

As an adult, James Madison was five feet four inches tall, and never weighed more than one hundred pounds. He was the shortest and slightest of all the presidents. His nose was scarred from once having been frostbitten. He always spoke in such a low voice that large audiences could barely hear him. Because of his shyness, as well as his small stature and weak voice, he often made a very bad first impression. In spite of these shortcomings, Madison became known as the father of the United States Constitution.

James Madison, the oldest of twelve children, was born in Port Conway, Virginia. Both his mother and father came from wealthy plantation families. His father was a justice of the peace, a landowner and farmer. His mother was the daughter of the owner of a tobacco warehouse.

James was a frail and sickly child. He had many playmates, most of whom were the children of his father's slaves. At night he often lay awake, afraid of the Indian raids in the mountain forests close by, their spine-chilling war whoops echoing through the valley. Both the companionship from his boyhood days and the trauma of the nights made lasting impressions on James. As an adult, he remained bitterly anti-Indian and emphatically anti-slavery.

James' father valued education for his children, though he had little schooling himself, and he taught his sons the obligations to community service that the planter class assumed. Besides studying with private tutors, James learned to read and write from his grandmother.

When she died, James' father enrolled him in Donald Robertson's boarding school seventy miles away.

In James' first year at the boarding school he studied English, Latin, and Greek. The open invitation to use the well-stocked library was exciting for this intellectually gifted student. It was quite an opportunity for James after living with the modest collection of books at Montpelier, most of which were devoted to farming and religion.

By the time Madison left Robertson's school in 1767 at age sixteen, he had read the works of Plato, Plutarch, and the other great philosophers in their original Greek. Books were, to Madison, like water to a seal — his natural element where he could dive in and feel at home. In later life he said of the scholarly schoolmaster at the Robertson School, "All I have been in life I owe largely to that man."

Madison was a homebody, preferring books to the rough sports and play of hearty boys. Shy and thoughtful, he learned to read French and Spanish while he was quite young, and he worked hard to master Greek and Latin. Some around him thought it would have been better for James to have mixed a good deal of play with his hard study.

As Madison approached college age, he began to suffer from disturbing seizures. This caused his parents to have some doubts about sending James away to college. Nevertheless, at age eighteen Madison entered the College of New Jersey at Princeton. He was a dedicated student and a natural scholar who retained and applied everything he learned. He studied very hard, sometimes sleeping only five hours a night. James completed the regular coursework in two years. At Princeton he studied Locke and Montesquieu, and like Thomas Jefferson, he was able to apply their philosophies to the reality of the American situation.

After receiving his Bachelor of Arts degree in 1771 at the age of twenty, James considered becoming a minister; he remained at Princeton for another year to study Hebrew and ethics. However, a weak speaking voice prevented him from taking up a career in the ministry, and he returned home in doubt about his future. His studies and extracurricular interests had also weakened his physical condition. For more than two years his deteriorating health left him tense, depressed and uncertain.

Madison studied law sporadically to broaden his knowledge, but he never gained admission to the bar. At age twenty-three he became a delegate to the Virginia Convention, and in 1776 he became a member of the Virginia House of Delegates. He went on to become the youngest delegate in the Continental Congress. This led to him becoming a U.S. Representative from Virginia, and then Secretary of State under President Thomas Jefferson. It was from this position that he was elected as the fourth President of the United States.

More Information About James Madison	
State Represented	Virginia
Party Affiliation	Democratic-Republican
School(s) Attended	Princeton University
Siblings	First of Twelve Children
Occupation(s)	Lawyer
Pet(s)	Macaw
Hobbies	Reading, Playing Chess
Political Particulars	Helped frame the Bill of Rights; Father of the U.S. Constitution
States in Union During Teenage Years	Zero

JAMES MONROE

Fifth President of the United States
Lived: 1758 – 1831   Served: 1817 – 1825

Although James Monroe is said to have lacked brilliance and a nimble mind, he did have a rare ability to put men at ease thanks to his courtesy, frankness, and what his contemporaries saw as his essential kindness of heart. He was able to partially overcome an early shyness, but remained markedly low-key and reserved throughout his life, especially around strangers.

James, the oldest of five children, was born in Virginia. His father was a circuit judge and a farmer who owned his own land. He brought home many pamphlets and newspapers read throughout the colonies, which made exciting reading for young James, who did not have access to many books.

James' mother taught him and his siblings to read and write. She used what was available as learning tools – she based the children's arithmetic lessons on the practical matters of farming and their father's construction business. Until James went to school he did not have any friends except for his brothers and sisters. He spent much of his time alone, but he always found interesting things to do.

As soon as James was old enough to hold a rifle, his father taught him how to shoot and hunt. There were also chores to do, lessons to study, a horse to ride, woods to roam and a stream in which to fish.

There was one chore James really disliked. He was responsible for plucking goose feathers on the family farm – and the geese did not like being plucked. The geese tried to bite the hands that pulled their feathers. Like most colonial families, the Monroes used the feathers for stuffing pillows, quilts and mattresses. Only when a goose was very old did they use it for food.

When James was seven-years-old, he was profoundly influenced by national events. He saw how angry his father was because of a new law that was forced on the American colonists by the British. The Stamp Act required that colonists attach a special stamp to all legal documents and business papers. Anyone who did not buy and use these stamps faced punishment. Until then James had never heard his parents say anything against the English government, but this was the first time the British placed a direct tax on the American colonies. Even as a child Monroe was impressed by the strong feelings and bravery shown by the protesters. He admired George Washington for identifying the colonists as Americans rather than British subjects. That alone took a lot of courage.

James did not go to school until he was eleven-years-old. He attended Campbelltown Academy, which was regarded as the best school in Virginia at the time. There were only twenty-five students at the academy. The lessons were difficult and James had to work very hard, especially at Latin and mathematics, but he still found time for fun.

He enjoyed walking the several miles to school each day, through woods and over streams. James always carried his rifle, but not because of any danger. There was a good chance of spotting a rabbit, squirrel or game bird along the way, and he liked practicing his shooting and being able to bring home food.

In 1774, when James was sixteen, he left the academy. It was a turning point in his life. His father had just died, leaving the children orphaned – James' mother had passed away a few years earlier. Although his uncle, Judge Joseph Jones, was not in charge of the Monroe estate, he looked after the estate until James reached the age of twenty-one.

Judge Jones felt that James had a bright future in Virginia politics. The boy was intelligent, well-liked, and trustworthy. The Judge was sure that with those qualities, and a good education, his nephew would succeed. The Judge's plan, to which James agreed, was that the teenager would attend William and Mary College to study law. James applied to the college and was immediately accepted. Although he didn't have many years of formal schooling, he had learned a great deal in a short time.

James Monroe

While attending college, James closely followed state politics; at that time the Virginia Assembly was talking treason. Patrick Henry was thundering out words of defiance against England in nearby Richmond, and the whole country was like an erupting volcano. James was a proud American and, young as he was, it was hard for him to stay in school while his country was at war for freedom.

In 1776, at the age of eighteen, Monroe dropped out of college and enlisted in the Continental Army. After basic training, James and the seven-hundred-man regiment marched to join General George Washington in the Revolutionary War. That Christmas Monroe was among those crossing the Delaware with Washington to take part in the famous Battle of Trenton. There Lieutenant Monroe helped lead a bold charge against the British to capture two three-pound cannons that were about to be turned against them. In the raid he was severely wounded in the shoulder and was carried from battle. He would have bled to death if it were not for the immediate attention of Doctor John Riker. For his heroism, Monroe was promoted to captain.

In 1777 James took part in battles at Brandywine and Germantown and was promoted to major. His exemplary service during the Revolution earned him the lasting gratitude of his commander-in-chief. "He has, in every instance, maintained the reputation of a brave, active and sensible officer," General Washington wrote.

At age twenty Monroe was promoted to lieutenant colonel and was sent to recruit troops in Virginia. Although he failed to meet his goal, the experience greatly influenced his future career. It brought him into contact with Thomas Jefferson, then Governor of Virginia. Monroe began to practice law under Jefferson's guidance, and became his political disciple and lifelong friend.

Although he never attended law school, Monroe's training under Thomas Jefferson enabled him to be admitted to the Virginia Bar. At the same time, he became a member of the Continental Congress. James went on to become Minister to France, a U.S. Senator, Governor of Virginia, Secretary of State and Secretary of War under President Madison, before becoming the fifth President of the United States.

More Information About James Monroe	
State Represented	Virginia
Party Affiliation	Democratic-Republican
School(s) Attended	William and Mary College
Number of Siblings	First of Five Children
Occupation(s)	Lawyer, Army Officer
Hobbies	Hunting, Horseback Riding
Political Particulars	Negotiated the Missouri Compromise; wrote the Monroe Doctrine
States in Union During Teenage Years	Zero

JOHN QUINCY ADAMS

Sixth President of the United States
Lived: 1767 – 1848   Served: 1825 – 1829

John Quincy Adams was the first president who was the son of a former president. His father was John Adams, the second President of the United States. It would be another 175 years before this happened again, when George W. Bush became president.

John was the second child and oldest son in a family of five. One of his brothers, also an attorney, died of alcoholism at the age of thirty.

Adams was a brilliant, precocious boy who grew up amid a lot of excitement. From their nearby family farm, John and his mother witnessed the Battle of Bunker Hill in 1775. School was suspended in Braintree, Massachusetts during the American Revolution, so young John learned the fundamentals at home under the tutelage of his parents and a pair of his father's law clerks.

John was a serious, thoughtful boy who preferred hearing the old folks talk over playing with his schoolmates. Before he was seven-years-old he had become a faithful reader of the Patriot Press. By age ten he was already reading Shakespeare. John did the work of a man long before he ceased being a boy. Like his father, he was honest, fearless and obstinate. To the day of his death nothing scared him, and nothing turned him from his course. He was similar in temperament to his father, and their careers and viewpoints were remarkably parallel.

Adams was ten-years-old when his father was sent as Ambassador to France, and John went along. It was a long and stormy voyage, and on the way they were chased by a British war vessel and had a desperate battle with pirates. His father wanted to help the sailors fight, but the captain wouldn't let him.

John received his first formal education at an academy outside Paris, where he studied with the grandson of Benjamin Franklin. He learned fencing, dance, music and art, in addition to the classics. With his father, John worked through problems in algebra, geometry, trigonometry and calculus. By the time he returned to America, Adams had mastered Latin, Greek, French, Dutch and Spanish. On the way back home, at age twelve, he was giving English language lessons to the French Ambassador.

It wasn't long before John went abroad again. This time, at the age of thirteen, he became the private secretary of Francis Dana, the United States envoy to Russia. John was the youngest person ever to hold such a high office. He stayed in Russia for over a year, and then came back alone, traveling through Sweden and Denmark. Circumstances brought him to Holland, where he went to school at The Hague. He had been getting his schooling in bits and pieces all along, but at this school of courts there was much to learn.

No sooner had John settled down with his books than his father reappeared and moved him to France, where he could keep a closer eye on him. There John watched the signing of the Treaty of Paris between the United States and Great Britain, which ended the American Revolution. Before he was eighteen John was able to hold his own in discussions with Benjamin Franklin, Thomas Jefferson and his father. Whomever he encountered, American or foreign, he could speak with him in his own language.

In 1785, before John was eighteen, his father was appointed Minister to England. Young Adams had another opportunity to travel abroad, but instead he chose to go to school full time at Harvard University. In his spare time he learned shorthand and read voraciously — everything from ancient history to popular literature. He graduated with honors at the age of twenty, and began to study law.

John opened his own law office in 1790 at the age of twenty-three, but he did not do well attracting clients. President Washington appointed him as Minister to the Netherlands and Prussia, and then Adams was elected to the Massachusetts State Senate. The following year he was elected to the U.S. Senate for two terms. He went on to become Minister to Russia, prior to becoming the chief negotiator of the Treaty of Ghent, which ended the War of 1812. He became Secretary of State under President Monroe, before becoming the sixth President of the United States.

John Quincy Adams was the only president to serve as a U.S. Representative in the United States Congress after his term as president. He did so for seventeen years.

More Information About John Quincy Adams	
State Represented	Massachusetts
Party Affiliation	Democratic-Republican
School(s) Attended	Harvard
Number of Siblings	Second of Five Children
Occupation(s)	Lawyer
Hobbies	Hunting, Horseback Riding, Reading, Swimming, Writing
Political Particulars	Chief negotiator of Treaty of Ghent (Ending War of 1812)
States in Union During Teenage Years	Zero

ANDREW JACKSON

Seventh President of the United States
Lived: 1767 – 1845   Served: 1829 – 1837

Andrew Jackson was the youngest of three children. His father, a linen weaver and farmer in Ireland, moved his family to South Carolina, and he died in an untimely accident before Andrew was born. Fortunately there were many relatives and neighbors nearby to help the family cope with their tragic loss. It wasn't unusual to find large families living close together on the frontier, and these extended families worked together, always willing to lend a hand. Both of Andrew's older brothers died fighting in the American Revolution.

Andrew was a freckle-faced youngster who had blue eyes and thick messy red hair. At the age of five he went to a terrible school in a log cabin out in the woods. He learned to read, but he never became a good speller; his writing was never great, but he was able to learn simple arithmetic. He was an active youngster who hated to sit still for very long. While it was always a battle to keep him in school, he learned very quickly, and often on his own.

Andrew picked up every newspaper he could find and read it from front to back. This was a habit that lasted a lifetime. At age eight he was writing in script. By the time he was nine he was already a public reader — since so many of the settlers couldn't read at all, newspapers that brought word of events around the nation were read out loud for them by young Andrew. That same year the Declaration of Independence was signed, and Andrew had the unique opportunity to read it to the public.

When he wasn't reading, he was busy playing outdoors. He became a very good horseman at an early age. It didn't matter how wild the animal, Andrew would mount up and take-off. If he wasn't riding, he was running and jumping. He would jump fences, climb rocks and trees, race and play games of tag.

He also had a quick temper. If any of the boys teased him about anything, a fight was not far off; it didn't matter how strong or big the other boy might be. Though he didn't always win his fights, Andrew never gave up.

During the Revolutionary War, a British Colonel and his horsemen attacked and destroyed much of South Carolina. Andrew's oldest brother Hugh was among those who fought the colonel, and he was cruelly killed. When Andrew heard of this he wanted to avenge his brother's death, but he was too young to take up the sword and fight. His mother took the children and fled to safety in Charlotte, North Carolina, where Andrew was placed with a family to earn his room and board doing servant's work.

In 1778 Andrew took part in a cattle drive. Since it was his first drive, he had the difficult job of riding in the rear to make sure there were no stragglers. It was a big responsibility for an eleven- year-old. Andrew loved living out in the open with the men and listening to their stories.

Because his mother had her heart set on her youngest son becoming a minister, Andrew received a better education than his older brothers. Starting at age eight he learned the fundamentals and studied the classics. However, despite his mother's wishes, Andrew was never a good student and never had any inclination to enter the clergy. He stayed in school on and off until he was thirteen. At that point national events were increasing in urgency, and they would change young Andrew's life forever.

In mid-July of 1780, at age thirteen, Andrew Jackson became a member of the American Army. He became a *mounted orderly*, a carrier of messages. He was now a Patriot. It wasn't long before he and his brother Robert were given muskets and were expected to fight like any other soldier.

When the British forces seized the town of Charlotte, they took Andrew and his brother captive. As a prisoner of war, Andrew was as strong and bold as many much older men. One day, a British officer ordered Andrew to clean his muddy boots. Andrew, full of courage and a fighting spirit, refused. "I'm a prisoner of war," he told the officer, "not your servant." When Andrew refused the officer's order, the officer slashed Jackson with a saber, cutting his left arm to the bone and leaving a gash on his forehead. The officer then tried to get Andrew's brother to polish his boots. Robert also rebelled and was beaten. The boys' wounds went unattended during a forty-mile march to a military prison, and they contracted smallpox. Through some stroke of luck their mother was able to arrange a prisoner exchange with the British. Drenched by rain through the long walk home, both boys became delirious. Robert died, but Andrew survived thanks to his incredible stamina.

Not long before his mother died of cholera, she advised Andrew to make friends, be honest, and fight for his convictions if he wanted to survive. His mother had set her personal feelings and safety aside to do everything she could to support her children, and that quality was something Andrew would always remember.

His mother's death left fifteen-year-old Andrew an orphan, and he was forced to move around from one relative's home to another. He tried working, but his heart wasn't in it. He tried school again, but that didn't last long either. He was too restless – he kept thinking that if his family had survived, his life would be better.

Jackson started to learn the saddler's trade, but did not stick to it very long. He was free from any restraint or home influence and was vulnerable to all of society's evils. Angry at the world that left him without a family, Andrew became unruly – attending horse races, gambling and doing many things a young boy should not do. Nothing seemed to inspire him. At just sixteen-years-old, his bitterness over the war plagued him and he became even more wild and undisciplined. No one expected a boy like that would ever come to any good – such boys seldom did. They were more likely to end up in prison. Jackson often spoke about his narrow escape from vice.

As luck would have it, Andrew inherited some money from his grandfather who had recently died in Ireland. For the first time in his life he had options. He could go back and put the old farm in shape. Or he could choose to go to college or law school.

The first thing Andrew did with his inheritance was buy several fine suits and walk proudly through town. Instead of settling down and using his money wisely, he met a group of young people and began to drift with them. Much of their time was spent at the racetrack. Andrew bet heavily and enjoyed every minute of it. His life had no plan; he had absolutely no concern for himself or his future.

Within a very short period of time, all of his inheritance was gone. He couldn't even pay for his room.

In 1784, at the age of seventeen, he left his hometown for good. He decided to teach school, but that didn't last long. Andrew persuaded a middle-aged lawyer in North Carolina to take him on as a law student. In those days, especially on the frontier, students didn't have to attend college or law school to become an attorney. They could assist a certified lawyer, and when they were ready, take an exam given by a judge.

Although Andrew studied hard, he continued to gamble, drink and chase women. He also attended cockfights where roosters fought to the death. He still had a wild streak. He also had a charming quality that drew people to him. Andrew Jackson impressed people – once they met him, they remembered him.

After spending two years studying law, he went to work for a well-known lawyer in Nashville, Tennessee. At age twenty, he qualified as an attorney. Two judges concluded that Jackson was a person of unblemished moral character, and was competent in his knowledge of the law.

Although Andrew Jackson never went to college, he went on to become a U.S. Congressman, a major general in the army, Governor of the Florida Territory, a U.S. Senator, a judge, and the seventh President of the United States.

More Information About Andrew Jackson	
Born	South Carolina
State Represented	Tennessee
Party Affiliation	Democratic-Republican
School(s) Attended	Studied sporadically
Siblings	Third of Three Children
Occupation(s)	Lawyer
Hobbies	Gambling, Horseback Riding, Reading
Political Particulars	Nicknamed "Old Hickory"; Hero of War of 1812
States in Union During Teenage Years	Zero

MARTIN VAN BUREN

Eighth President of the United States
Lived: 1782 – 1862   Served: 1837 – 1841

Martin Van Buren was born in Kinderhook,* New York, a small village twenty miles south of Albany. Both of his parents came from Holland. He was the third of five children (he had an older brother and sister, and two younger brothers). His mother was a widow and had three children from her first marriage, one of whom became a congressman. Martin's father was a poor truck farmer who, with the help of slaves, worked very hard to make ends meet. He was also a tavern-keeper and served as town clerk.

Although relatively poor, Van Buren's parents recognized the value of a good education. Martin went to the local village school and then to Kinderhook Academy; after school he delivered farm produce and helped in his father's tavern. Martin was an active boy who was shrewd and had plenty of his father's good nature.

Martin learned about politics inside his father's tavern, where the neighbors gathered to talk over events of the day. There's no doubt the quick-witted boy picked up many useful lessons from commoners, lawyers, and politicians alike. Even as a youngster, Martin relished listening to the political conversations of men like Alexander Hamilton and Aaron Burr.

Van Buren's early education was limited to a few years at the academy. He learned the basics of reading and writing at a dreary, poorly lit schoolhouse in his native village (there would be no electricity for another one hundred years). He excelled in composition and speaking. His formal education ended when he was fourteen-years-old – Martin's father did not send him to college. He may have thought too much learning would do his son more harm than good.

At age fourteen Martin was apprenticed to a village lawyer, Francis Sylvester. He swept out the office, lit the log fire, ran errands, patiently read law books and eagerly read every journal he could find on Jeffersonian politics.

He quickly showed great talent and was allowed to work in court. When he was only sixteen- years-old, Van Buren was given a case to try before a justice of the peace and a jury in his hometown. Opposing him was an older lawyer of great experience and ability, who had won almost every case he tried. But Martin, undaunted, went into court and was a source of great amusement. He was so short that when the trial began, his friends lifted him up on a table to address the jury (he was only five feet six inches tall, the second shortest president next to James Madison who was five feet four inches tall). Despite his youth and small stature, Martin had thoroughly prepared his case and spoke so eloquently that he won. The boy was rewarded that day with a silver half-dollar. He soon became a familiar sight in the village court.

By the time he was eighteen-years-old, his precise legal mind had brought him much local renown. He still took time to campaign successfully for Jefferson, so he was sent as a delegate to a regional caucus. In 1801, at age nineteen, Martin entered a New York City law office and began barely earning a living. Van Buren was admitted to the bar at age twenty-one, and he then opened his own law office.

Martin was good-natured and had a smiling and kindly manner that brought him many friends. He was a hard-worker and loved books, reading everything that came his way, which helped him learn many things apart from law.

Martin Van Buren went on to become a New York State Senator, a U.S. Senator, Governor of New York, Ambassador to Great Britain, Secretary of State and Vice President under President Jackson, and the eighth President of the United States.

* Martin Van Buren gave us the word "okay" or "OK," which was an abbreviation for the name of his hometown in New York – Old Kinderhook. The "O.K. Club" was a Democratic organization formed to support President Van Buren for re-election. The word "O.K." became commonly used to mean "all correct," or to endorse or approve.

More Information About Martin Van Buren	
State Represented	New York
Party Affiliation	Democratic-Republican
School(s) Attended	Early schooling in Old Kinderhook, did not attend college
Siblings	Third of Five Children
Occupation(s)	Lawyer
Hobbies	Public Speaking, Reading
Political Particulars	Nicknamed "Little Magician"
States in Union During Teenage Years	Sixteen

WILLIAM HENRY HARRISON

Ninth President of the United States
Lived: 1773 – 1841   Served: March, 1841 – April, 1841

William Henry Harrison, the youngest of seven children (four girls and three boys), was born on his father's plantation in Virginia in 1773. His parents came from prominent Virginia families, and his father, Benjamin Harrison, served in both Continental Congresses and signed the Declaration of Independence.

Harrison grew up during the American Revolution. When he was nearly eight-years-old, a unit of Hessian troops (German mercenaries) and American Tories (loyalists who supported the British) under the command of General Benedict Arnold, attacked the Harrison home. Although the Harrisons learned of the advance in time to flee to safety, the Tories stripped their home of its furnishings, slaughtered their livestock, and carried off their slaves and horses.

William and his siblings received their early education at home from tutors because there were no schools nearby. When he was fourteen, his father sent him to Hampden-Sydney College for pre-medical instruction. He studied classical languages, geography, history, mathematics and rhetoric; he especially liked military history, and was a founder of the campus literary society. He left before graduation because his father became annoyed with the school's religious teachings.

When William was seventeen, he was transferred to an academy in South Hampton County, where he remained briefly before becoming an apprentice to Dr. Andrew Leiper. But his father was again unhappy because his son had taken up with a "bad crowd" – abolitionists. Abolitionists wanted to see all the slaves freed, and the Harrison wealth was based in large part on labor from the slaves. His father was quite upset, and a short time later William transferred to the University of Pennsylvania Medical School, where he studied under Dr. Benjamin Rush.

While he was at school, his father died. William inherited some land, but most of the family money went to the eldest son, Benjamin. Following his father's wishes, William planned to continue his studies at the medical school. But Benjamin refused to continue paying for his brother's schooling, so William decided to quit his medical education and join the military.

At age eighteen, Harrison's love of adventure and his anger about the cruelties being committed by the Indians inspired him to enlist in the army. George Washington, a friend of his father's, approved of the decision. William became a professional soldier, rising from ensign to major general. After a distinguished career in the military, he became a U.S. Congressman. He went on to serve for twelve years as the Governor of the Indiana Territory, as a U.S. Senator and as the ninth President of the United States.

William Henry Harrison served the shortest term as president: he died after being in office for only one month. His inauguration was a cold and windy day in March. Standing bareheaded, without gloves or an overcoat, the sixty-eight-year-old president – the oldest man elected president until Ronald Reagan – read a meandering inaugural address that lasted for an hour and forty minutes. Three weeks later he got caught in a torrential rain, came down with a cold, and ended up with pneumonia. A week later he was pronounced dead. He was the first president to die in office.

More Information About William Henry Harrison	
Born	Virginia
State Represented	Ohio
Party Affiliation	Whig
School(s) Attended	Hampden-Sydney College, University of Pennsylvania Medical School
Siblings	Seventh of Seven Children
Occupation(s)	Army Officer
Hobbies	Horseback Riding
Political Particulars	Hero of the Battle of Tippecanoe and the War of 1812
States in Union During Teenage Years	Fifteen

JOHN TYLER

Tenth President of the United States
Lived: 1790 – 1862   Served: 1841 – 1845

John Tyler was the first vice president to become President of the United States upon the death of another president.

John, the sixth child in a family of eight, was born on his family's plantation in Charles City County, Virginia. His father, a lawyer, judge and governor, wanted his son to be well educated and study law. His mother died of a stroke when he was seven-years-old.

It is said that, as an infant, John gazed into the night sky and stretched his arms up to grab the shining moon. Seeing this, his mother remarked, "This child is destined to become President of the United States, because his wishes fly so high." Unfortunately, she died so young that she did not live to see her prophecy fulfilled.

Unlike some other presidents, John's early home surroundings were very good. He came from the old planter class with its elite training and high social standing. Very early his father and mother began teaching him at home. When he entered school, he already knew how to read and write, and was very fond of books.

A housekeeper who helped raise John described him as being gentle like his mother, with silky brown hair and bright blue eyes. As a boy, he was generally good-natured. Even as a young man he had graceful manners, was a good speaker, and was ready to be friends with everyone. As he grew up, like his father, he wrote poetry and played the violin.

Bright and headstrong, Tyler also inherited a fiery spirit from his father. When he was eleven, he led a rebellion of students against their tyrannical Scottish schoolmaster. The teacher was an intelligent man, well versed in his subjects, but he used birch switches from the swamp to whip the children mercilessly. The parents and guardians of his pupils never questioned his authority. One day, under young Tyler's leadership, the boys threw the teacher down, tied him up and locked him in a closet. When John's father found out the reason for the rebellion, he had no sympathy for the cruel schoolmaster.

John soon showed that he was a boy with more than ordinary abilities. He had a quick mind, an excellent memory, loved reading, and got a good start in his happy home with his parents. He was only twelve when he entered William and Mary College. Tyler was interested in ancient history, law and political science. Besides the classics, he studied English Literature and economics. A good student, he studied so hard that he graduated with honors at the age of seventeen.

Taught to play the fiddle by his father, John had visions of being an accomplished violinist. However, it soon became apparent that law, not music, was to be his career. Upon graduation he returned to Charles City County where he studied law, first with his father and his cousin Chancellor Samuel Tyler, and then at the Richmond office of Edmund Randolph, the first U.S. Attorney General. In 1809, at the age of nineteen, John was admitted to the bar.

John Tyler went on to become a member of the Virginia House of Delegates, a U.S. Congressman, Governor of Virginia, a U.S. Senator and Vice President. Upon the death of President William Henry Harrison, he became President of the United States.

Tyler decided to retire rather than run again for the presidency. During his retirement, starting at age fifty-five, he fathered seven more children with his second wife Julia Gardiner, making a grand total of fourteen children. His first wife, Leticia Christian, died while he was in office.

John died while a member of the Confederate Congress, and was denounced in the North as a traitor.

More Information About John Tyler	
State Represented	Virginia
Party Affiliation	Whig
School(s) Attended	William and Mary College
Siblings	Sixth of Eight Children
Occupation(s)	Lawyer
Hobbies	Playing Violin, Reading
Political Particulars	Nicknamed "His Accidency"
States in Union During Teenage Years	Seventeen

JAMES KNOX POLK

Eleventh President of the United States
Lived: 1795 – 1849   Served: 1845 – 1849

James K. Polk was by nature an introvert, with few genuinely close friends, but out of political necessity he forced himself to mingle. He was very ambitious, a classic overachiever. His passionate drive was due in part to his poor health growing up and his discomfort at being shorter than others his own age. To compensate for a lack of brilliance and charisma, he drove himself ruthlessly, exploiting the energy and abilities he did possess to an extent that few men could match.

James, the oldest of ten children, was born on the family farm in Mecklenburg County, North Carolina. He had five brothers and four sisters – three of his brothers died in their twenties, one of alcoholism at the age of twenty-eight. Their father was a surveyor, a prosperous farmer and land speculator. He eventually owned thousands of acres of land and more than fifty slaves. James' mother was a devout Presbyterian. She impressed upon her family the value of religion and education, but when it came time for James to be baptized his father refused to say he was a Presbyterian and the ceremony was never completed.

When James was ten-years-old, his family moved to Tennessee. It was a grueling and exciting journey of nearly five hundred miles by wagon over rugged terrain. The rigors of frontier life were hard on James' weak constitution; he was a small and sickly boy. His parents spared him many of the chores done by most farm boys, but when he could he worked hard chopping down trees, building fences and planting crops. He fared poorly in the rough and tumble sports common among Tennessee youth.

Polk's father took his bright but frail son on his long surveying expeditions, where James usually kept close to camp, cooking and tending to the horses. When James was able, they would climb mountains, wade through gorges and had narrow escapes from Indians.

The sense of purpose that drove James throughout his life owed more to his mother than his father. His father had planned for him to be a surveyor and storekeeper, in addition to being a farmer. But what James and his mother wanted more than anything, was more schooling. Until James was seventeen he had no formal education, but he enjoyed studying. He then went to public schools and loved reading. His mother knew that a boy who was willing to learn and desired to find good books was likely to succeed. His mother did a lot to help him, and through her guidance James became a very good student.

James suffered from gallstones, and at age seventeen the pain got so bad that he went to Kentucky to undergo what was then a very risky operation. With only liquor to dull the pain (this was before the discovery of anesthesia or antiseptics), Polk survived the operation to remove the gallstones. He was able to return to Tennessee with improved health.

After James was well, his father put him to work in a general store, but he was unhappy with that kind of life. A few years later, at the age of twenty-one, Polk's father sent him to the University of North Carolina, Chapel Hill, where he could get a better education. While at the university, James received an education in the classics, with an emphasis on Greek, Latin and philosophy. He especially liked mathematics and was among the best in his class. He also enjoyed public speaking and debate, and he was chosen as president of the Dialectic Society. He joined regularly in their debates, and on one occasion he argued that foreigners should not be permitted to hold public office.

James graduated at the top of his class at the age of twenty-three. He had studied so hard that his health was affected and he needed a good rest before he could begin his study of the law. He became a lawyer with very pleasant manners and an easy speaking style. His practice was profitable, largely because his friendly demeanor came from the heart.

James Polk

James Polk went on to become a U.S. Congressman and Speaker of the House, the Governor of Tennessee and, at age forty-nine, the youngest President of the United States to date. Polk was the first "dark horse" candidate, not getting the nomination of the Democratic Party until the ninth ballot. When Polk declared war on Mexico, Abraham Lincoln denounced the conflict as an act of U.S. aggression, fearing slavery would expand. While it did lead to bitter disagreements between North and South, the victory over Mexico gave the United States California, Nevada, Utah, Wyoming, Colorado, Texas, New Mexico and Arizona. Polk is considered the greatest one-term president and the last strong president before the Civil War. Unfortunately his hard work as president undermined his health, and he died soon after he left office.

More Information About James K. Polk	
Born	North Carolina
State Represented	Tennessee
Party Affiliation	Democrat
School(s) Attended	University of North Carolina, Chapel Hill
Siblings	First of Ten Children
Occupation(s)	Lawyer
Hobbies	Reading
Political Particulars	Expansionist who promoted "Manifest Destiny"
States in Union During Teenage Years	Eighteen

ZACHARY TAYLOR

Twelfth President of the United States
Lived: 1784 – 1850   Served: 1849 – 1850

Zachary Taylor had long gangly arms, a thick torso, and short bowed legs. A high forehead and a long nose dominated his thin face. He was farsighted and walleyed (his eyes turned outward away from his nose and showed more than a normal amount of white), he wore reading glasses and often squinted. He dressed sloppily, wearing whatever was most comfortable – even as a soldier he typically wore a hodgepodge of civilian and military dress.

Zachary, the third child in a family of nine children (seven sons and two daughters), was born on a relative's estate in Orange County, Virginia. After a few months, he and his family moved to a wilderness settlement near Louisville, Kentucky, where they began to farm. They could hear the howling wolves and see the Indians harass the settlers from their new home.

Zachary's father had won acclaim as a soldier during the Revolutionary War, and as a reward for his military efforts Colonel Taylor was given six thousand acres of land. He became not only a farmer, but also a justice of the peace and a customs collector. He helped write the laws when Kentucky was granted statehood and served in the state legislature. Zachary's mother was well-educated considering the times. The little that has been written about her says that her major accomplishment was raising a boy who learned to read even as he was dreaming of becoming a soldier.

With good educations themselves, Zachary's parents were determined that their children would be equally well-schooled. Unfortunately there were no schools where they settled in Kentucky, so after doing their own tutoring for a while, the Taylors hired a wandering schoolteacher, and then an Irish teacher who set up a school in the neighborhood.

Zachary, a bright, active boy with an independent mind, grew up working very hard on his father's farm. He was brave and was never afraid of wild animals or Indians. Zachary soon learned to rely on himself and to defend the weak. He loved to ride horseback, and at age seventeen he swam the breadth of the Ohio River to Indiana and back again in the chill of early spring.

Zachary was sent to an academy in Louisville, and although he never acquired polished skills in spelling and writing, he could nonetheless convey his thoughts with purpose and force, an ability that would prove useful throughout his life. Zachary never went to college, but he did enjoy reading. He could not get enough of adventure stories and tales of military heroes and their battles.

His admiration for his father, and the older man's willingness to share endless Revolutionary War experiences, no doubt fanned Zachary's early interest in soldiering. He wanted to join the army and fight the Indians, who were attacking frontier towns, killing people and burning farm houses. At age twenty-three Zachary accepted a commission as a first lieutenant in the U.S. Army, and he served as an officer for the next forty years.

Taylor went on to become a captain during the War of 1812, a colonel during the Black Hawk War, a brigadier general during the second Seminole War, and was promoted to major general during the Mexican War, in which he became a national hero.

Zachary Taylor was the first president elected to office with no previous political experience. He was only in office for a year and a half before he got sick after eating cherries and milk at a July 4th celebration. He died of a gastrointestinal condition five days later. He was the second president to die in office.

More Information About Zachary Taylor	
Born & Lived	Born in Virginia, Lived in Kentucky
State Represented	Louisiana
Party Affiliation	Whig
School(s) Attended	Studied at home & at academy in Kentucky; did not attend college
Siblings	Third of Nine Children
Occupation(s)	Army Officer
Hobbies	Horseback Riding, Swimming, Gifted Marksman
Political Particulars	Nationalist, nicknamed "Old Rough & Ready"
States in Union During Teenage Years	Seventeen

MILLARD FILLMORE

Thirteenth President of the United States
Lived: 1800 – 1874   Served: 1850 – 1853

Millard Fillmore, the second child in a family of three girls and six boys, was born in a log cabin in central New York. His parents were poor but hard-working farmers. Millard did his share of farm chores: clearing fields, plowing, harvesting and chopping wood; in his spare time he enjoyed hunting in the woods and fishing at the nearby lake. From his youth he was determined to one day leave the farm and make something of himself in the outside world.

Millard came from a humble home, where he had few advantages and there was not much opportunity for education. A bright child, and quick to learn when he could find the tools, he had little formal education. His mother taught him to read using a bible, a hymnbook and an almanac that she brought with her from Vermont. Millard saw no other books until he started attending school at age seventeen, and although he only went for short periods of time, he did learn some reading, spelling, geography, and arithmetic. Millard was a good-natured child who, despite his modest upbringing, never felt deprived because of the lack of books in his home, and he no doubt had a good time at play.

When Millard was fourteen, he was apprenticed to a cloth-maker one hundred miles from home. His master treated him so badly that Millard once threatened him with an ax. He disliked it there enough that he quit after four months. His father sent him to another cloth-dresser, and although Millard remained there for several years, he still did not care for the trade.

When a circulating library was formed in the community, Fillmore discovered the world of ideas, and he realized how little he really knew. His vocabulary was so weak that he had trouble understanding what he read, so he bought his first dictionary and mastered new words during his idle moments at the cloth mill. This also helped him learn a great deal about history, among other things. By age nineteen Millard had read enough to qualify as a part-time student at a local academy. An eager student, he was a favorite of his teacher Abigail Powers, whom he later married.

A short time later Millard's father arranged for him to study law with a judge. Fillmore was so ecstatic at the news that he wept openly. At the end of a two-month trial period, the judge invited Millard to continue as his clerk on a permanent basis, provided he was able to free himself of his indenture to the cloth-maker. Realizing that the boy had little money, the judge offered to lend him funds and find him extra work. Millard taught school for a few months to earn some cash, and then he bought up his indenture for thirty dollars. (Indentured servitude, along with slavery, was ultimately outlawed in 1865 with the passing of the thirteenth amendment to the United States Constitution.)

At the judge's law office Fillmore was responsible for overseeing the tenant farmers, a task he disliked because at times he was expected to evict poor families. After a couple of years, he abruptly quit after an argument with the judge. Millard then joined his parents and taught school briefly, while he continued to study law; he never went to college, but he passed the bar at age twenty-three.

Millard Fillmore is known as a true exemplar of the American dream, rising from a log cabin to wealth and the White House because of sheer determination. He served as a New York State Assemblyman, a U.S. Congressman, and vice president before he became president upon the death of President Zachary Taylor.

Fillmore amassed a personal library of some four thousand volumes, and as president he encouraged his wife to create the first permanent White House Library collection.

More Information About Millard Fillmore

State Represented	New York
Party Affiliation	Whig
Siblings	Second of Nine Children
School(s) Attended	Studied at home; did not attend college
Occupation(s)	Farmer, Lawyer
Hobbies	Hunting, Fishing, Reading
Political Particulars	Aided in passing the Compromise of 1850
States in Union During Teenage Years	Twenty-two

FRANKLIN PIERCE

Fourteenth President of the United States
Lived: 1804 – 1869   Served: 1853 – 1857

Franklin Pierce, his father's seventh child and the sixth of eight children in his father's second marriage, was born in a log cabin in New Hampshire. Franklin's father served in the Revolutionary War and became a brigadier general in the state militia. He also worked as a farmer, a tavern owner, sheriff, and two-term Governor of New Hampshire. Pierce's mother was very affectionate and tender, but she had a tendency toward mental depression and alcoholism, both of which Franklin inherited.

Franklin was a boy who took after his father – full of spirit and heart, fond of fun and outdoor sports, and well-liked among all who knew him. Growing up during the War of 1812, he loved hearing tales of combat from his older brother and from troops passing through the town where he lived. Pierce was a robust, active and devilish child, quick to pick a fight or pull a prank. With all his wildness, Franklin was a lovable boy with a natural courtesy and easy manner. These qualities served him well throughout his life.

Pierce learned to read and write at a brick schoolhouse in Hillsborough, New Hampshire. He was a bright student, and often spent his recess time tutoring slow learners. At age eleven Franklin was sent to an academy in nearby Hancock. Friends recalled that just after Franklin entered the school he got homesick and returned home on foot. His father put the runaway into a wagon, drove him halfway back to the academy and dropped him at the roadside... never saying a word. Franklin had to trudge the remaining seven miles back to school.

A year later he transferred to an academy in Francestown, New Hampshire, and then he moved to Phillips Exeter Academy. At the age of sixteen Pierce passed the entrance exam to gain admission to Bowdoin College in Brunswick, Maine, which required Latin composition, Greek translation, and knowledge of geography and math. He was very popular with his college classmates, but not with his teachers, because he wasted two years drinking and being lazy. During his sophomore year, he met two incoming freshmen, Nathaniel Hawthorne and Henry Wadsworth Longfellow (the future authors), with whom he formed lifelong friendships. The college boys formed a military company and made Franklin the captain. They committed so many lawless pranks that Franklin came close to being sent home in disgrace.

Pierce was an indifferent student until his junior year. He was absent often and fell to the bottom of his class. But he made a good friend in Zenas Caldwell, a studious and religious boy who gained such influence over Franklin that the wild young rebel began to study hard to make up for lost time. He eventually applied himself and, at age twenty, graduated fifth out of fourteen students in the class of 1824. In addition to classical languages and math, he studied history, chemistry, mineralogy and philosophy. He developed an intense interest in John Locke, finding particularly useful his *Essay Concerning Human Understanding*.

Upon graduation Franklin studied law, and at the age of twenty-three he was admitted to the bar. He became a good lawyer and, although he lost his first case, he showed his spirit by saying, "I will try nine hundred and ninety nine cases, if clients trust me: and if I fail, as I have today, I will try the thousandth." Men with that kind of attitude rarely fail.

In addition to serving two years in the military during the Mexican War, rising from private to brigadier general, Franklin Pierce was a member of the New Hampshire legislature, a U.S. Congressman, and a U.S. Senator. Pierce did not become a candidate for president until the thirty-fifth ballot. A true "dark horse," he was finally nominated on the forty-ninth ballot. Two months before he took office as the fourteenth President of the United States, Pierce and his wife Jane Means Appleton saw their eleven-year-old son killed in a train wreck.

More Information About Franklin Pierce

State Represented	New Hampshire
Party Affiliation	Democrat
Siblings	Sixth of eight children from second marriage
School(s) Attended	Bowdoin College
Occupation(s)	Lawyer
Hobbies	Reading, Paying pranks, Fishing
Political Particulars	Oversaw the passing of the Kansas-Nebraska Act to repeal the Missouri Compromise
States in Union During Teenage Years	Twenty-four

JAMES BUCHANAN

Fifteenth President of the United States
Lived: 1791 – 1868   Served: 1857 – 1861

James Buchanan was born with a peculiar eye disorder: one eye was nearsighted, the other farsighted. Additionally, the left eyeball was pitched higher in the socket than the right. To compensate, James developed the habit of cocking his head to one side and closing one eye. This gave him wryneck, a strange distinctive feature that forced his head to be habitually tilted to the left. If he was talking to someone or examining something close up, he would wink and shut the farsighted eye. If looking in the distance, he closed the nearsighted one. For reading he found it easier to focus with a candle in front of his eyes. He apparently coped well with the disorder, for he read much throughout his career, and did not wear glasses until the end of his life.

James, the oldest son of eleven children, was born in a log cabin deep in the mountains of Pennsylvania. His father prospered as a merchant and farmer, and he was in the public eye for many years serving as a justice of the peace. James worked in his father's frontier trading post, and while clerking there he learned arithmetic and bookkeeping, which helped him keep meticulous personal accounts throughout his life.

Largely self-educated, James' mother read a great deal, especially the bible and poetry. She was able to recite from memory large passages from the writings of John Milton and Alexander Pope. She encouraged the education of her children, and regularly tested their reasoning powers by engaging them in argument. Buchanan attributed much of his success to her. Three of her sons became lawyers, two of whom died at age twenty-two.

Young James was a good student with great promise. He learned the fundamentals at common schools and studied Latin and Greek at Old Stone Academy in Mercerburg, Pennsylvania. At age sixteen he was admitted as a junior to Dickinson College. He studied hard, taking a special interest in logic and metaphysics, but he also found time to get into trouble. Exactly what he did is unclear, but school officials definitely considered him a discipline problem. He was a rebellious kid, and he was expelled from Dickinson College at the end of his first year because of insubordination to his teachers and disorderly conduct. The school administration wrote his father at the end of the first year urging him to keep his devilish son home, but he intervened and got James reinstated. Buchanan thereupon pledged to reform, and he worked hard and behaved himself during his senior year.

His improved conduct did not completely satisfy the administration, however, for they pointedly denied a scholarship honor due him, even though he graduated at the top of his class. Mortified and disappointed, Buchanan considered boycotting commencement, but he relented and received his degree with the rest of the class of 1809, at only eighteen-years-old.

After he graduated, James applied himself diligently to reading law during the day and taking walks at night to contemplate what he had learned. He developed a skill for putting difficult legal concepts into everyday language. After studying law for the next three years, he began his law practice as an attorney in 1812.

Near the end of the War of 1812, the British plundered and burned Washington. When a town meeting was held in Lancaster, Pennsylvania, young Buchanan burst onto the stage and delivered his first public address, full of fire and patriotic spirit. As soon as he was done speaking, he volunteered for the military, but not in time to do any fighting.

James proved to be a gifted debater, and he went on to become a member of the Pennsylvania House of Representatives, a U.S. Representative, Minister to Russia in President Jackson's administration, a U.S. Senator, Secretary of State under President Polk, Minister to Great Britain in President Pierce's administration, and finally the fifteenth President of the United States.

Slavery was a paramount issue during his tenure as president. The Dred Scott decision had just been passed when he took office, which found slavery to be constitutional by a vote of 7-2. Although personally opposed to slavery on moral grounds, Buchanan felt constitutionally bound to uphold it. During his administration he also had to deal with the Depression of 1857 and the issue of secession that threatened to divide the nation. It was at the end of Buchanan's term as president when Fort Sumter was fired upon, beginning the Civil War. Although a northerner, Buchanan was a states rights advocate, and he blamed northern abolitionists for the Civil War.

James Buchanan is, to date, the only president who never married, and the only president from Pennsylvania.

More Information About James Buchanan

State Represented	Pennsylvania
Party Affiliation	Democrat
Siblings	First of Eleven
School(s) Attended	Dickinson College
Occupation(s)	Lawyer
Hobbies	Reading, Debating
Political Particulars	Believed that slavery was rooted in the U.S. Constitution
States in Union During Teen-age Years	Seventeen

ABRAHAM LINCOLN

Sixteenth President of the United States
Lived: 1809 – 1865   Served: 1861 – 1865

Some historians have said that Abraham Lincoln is the ugliest president the country has ever had. Yet many of the same historians claim him as this nation's greatest president. At six feet four inches, he was the tallest president; he weighed one hundred eighty pounds and had disproportionately long arms and legs, unusually long middle fingers and a sunken chest. Lincoln suffered from Marfan's syndrome, a hereditary disease that affects bone growth and heart function. He had a large wart on his right cheek and a scar over his right eye. His left eye was slightly higher than the right, and he had big bushy eyebrows. His careless dress habits further detracted from his appearance. However, Lincoln was comfortable with his homely appearance, and readily made fun of himself. Knowledge and self-confidence were always more important to him than how he looked.

Abraham Lincoln was born in a one-room, dirt-floored log cabin on a farm in the backwoods of Kentucky. He was the second of three children from his father (Thomas Lincoln) and mother (Nancy Hanks Lincoln); his stepmother, Thomas' second wife Sarah Bush Johnston, had three children of her own. Abraham's father worked as a frontier farmhand during most of his youth. He was known to be ignorant and lazy. He could neither read nor write, and was barely able to scrawl his name. He learned enough skill at woodworking to earn a living as a carpenter, and grew up literally without an education. He was no inspiration to his son at all, and when he died, Abraham did not attend the funeral. Lincoln's mother was an illegitimate child, and she was bright, though illiterate, pious, and close to her children.

The Lincoln's lived for two years on the farm where Abraham was born, and then they moved to a farm in Knob Creek. When Abraham could be spared from his chores, he went to a log schoolhouse, where he learned the basic skills of reading, writing and arithmetic. He and his family struggled for a living and for learning.

Abraham's father decided to move his family to Indiana, where a man could buy land directly from the government. Additionally, his father did not believe in slavery, and Indiana was not a slave state. The Lincolns found life harder in Indiana than in Kentucky – they arrived early in winter and needed shelter immediately. Father and son built a three-sided structure made of logs, and a fire on the fourth side burned night and day. Soon after finishing this shelter the seven-year-old boy and his father began to build a log cabin for their family.

Bears and other wild animals roamed the forests of the remote region in which they lived. Trees had to be cut and fields cleared so that a crop could be planted in the spring. At only eight-years-old, Abraham was large for his age and had enough strength to swing an ax. For as long as he lived in Indiana he was seldom without his ax – he later called it his "most useful instrument."

Abraham's mother died when he was only nine-years-old, of what the pioneers called "milk sickness," which was caused by consuming poison in the milk of cows that had eaten snakeroot. The cabin became dull and cheerless after the death of his mother. Sarah, his twelve-year-old sister, kept house as well as she could for more than a year. Then his father remarried and the new Mrs. Lincoln brought along her children, ages twelve, eight and five, and a wagonload of furniture and household goods. Abe's new mother was a good and wise woman, and her arrival at the cabin in Indiana ended the long months of loneliness. She took good care of him, and taught him how to make the most of the few things he had. She inspired him to dream of better things. She encouraged him to read and study, and that was what Abe liked most of all. There were not many books where he lived on the frontier, but he borrowed all he could lay his hands on, and read them over and over.

Presidents Were Teenagers Too

He studied all the difficult things he could find in books, from arithmetic and grammar, to surveying and law. Lincoln's formal schooling totaled less than one year, and he was the sixth president who never went to college, but he made extraordinary efforts to gain knowledge while working. He wrote on a shingle when he could not get paper, and by the light of a log fire when he could not get candles. He worked out questions in arithmetic on the back of a wooden shovel, and when it was full of figures he scraped them off and began again. He read and studied in the fields when he was not working, on woodpiles when he was chopping wood, or in the kitchen, rocking the cradle of any baby whose father or mother had a book to lend him. He would walk several miles for a book, and his favorites included: *Robinson Crusoe* by Daniel Defoe, *The Pilgrim's Progress* by John Bunyan, *Aesop's Fables,* a history of the United States, and a schoolbook or two. Books like Parson Weems' lyrical *Life of Washington* affected him deeply. When he borrowed the Weems' book and got it wet, he worked for three days on a farm to pay for it.

His favorite way to study was stretched out on an old chair in front of an open fire. He would read and write after the day's work was over, until he became one of the best scholars around. He learned a lot and, because of his determination, succeeded even without teachers. Although Abraham remembered little about his own mother, he had very fond words to say about her: "All that I am or hope ever to be I get from my mother. God bless her."

He worked on farms, split rails for farm fences, kept store and did all sorts of odd jobs for the farmers and their wives. And all the time he was working and having a good time, he kept studying. To help his father financially Abe hired himself out as a handyman. Some employers were not pleased with him. "He worked for me," said one employer, "but was always reading and thinking. I used to get mad at him for it. I would say he was awful lazy. He would laugh and talk, crack jokes and tell stories all the time.... He said to me... that his father taught him to work, but he never taught him to love it."

Even as a boy Abraham showed exceptional abilities as a speaker. He often amused himself and others by imitating some preacher or politician who had spoken in the neighborhood. Abraham's gift for telling stories made him a favorite among the men and boys. He read so much, and remembered things so well, that he could tell stories to make people laugh and stories to make people think. In spite of his youth, he was well known in his frontier neighborhood.

Abraham was the strongest boy in the countryside. He could mow the most, plow the deepest, split wood the best, toss the farthest, run the fastest, jump the highest and wrestle better than any boy or man in the neighborhood. But though he was strong, he was always kind, gentle, obliging, fair and helpful, and he was very well liked.

When Abraham was fourteen, his parents joined the Pigeon Creek Baptist Church. There was a bitter rivalry among Baptists and members of other denominations, but young Lincoln disliked any display of hostility among Christian people. This may explain why he never attended church regularly as an adult, yet he did become a man of deep religious beliefs. The bible was probably the only book his parents ever owned, and Abraham came to know it thoroughly. Biblical references and quotations enriched many of his later writings and speeches.

The first money he earned for himself was for rowing passengers to a steamboat in the middle of the Mississippi River. At age nineteen he helped take a flatboat loaded with farm produce to New Orleans. The trip gave him his first view of the world beyond his own community, and it was on this passage that Lincoln first saw the horror of slavery: Negroes in chains whipped and sold like cattle. In 1830 Abraham and his family left Indiana for Illinois. Abe served briefly as a captain in the Black Hawk War in 1832, and this leadership role fed his desire to enter politics.

At the age of twenty-two Abraham Lincoln ran for the Illinois State Legislature and lost. He then became a partner in a general store, which failed after a few years. After eventually being elected to the state legislature, where he served for eight years, he decided to study law and became an attorney. His law partner in Springfield, Illinois said of him, "His ambition was a little engine that knew no rest." After failing in his first attempt to run for the U.S. Congress, he took a brief hiatus from politics and married Mary Todd in 1842 – they had four sons together, only one of whom lived into adulthood. In 1846 Lincoln was elected to the U.S. House of Representatives. His next effort was as a candidate for vice president, but he also lost that election. In 1858 he ran and failed in his effort against Stephen Douglas for Illinois' U.S. Senate seat. But in the end his persistence paid off and he became the sixteenth President of the United States.

Lincoln's administration as president is well known for dealing with the Civil War, and his achievements – saving the Union and freeing the slaves – assured his continuing renown. On January 1,

1863, he issued the Emancipation Proclamation that declared forever free those slaves within the Confederacy and allowed blacks to serve in the military. Abraham Lincoln is known as one of the most charismatic and passionate speakers this nation has ever had, particularly during such a tumultuous time in United States history. Lincoln's place in history is defined, in no small part, by his eloquence as exemplified in the Gettysburg Address, delivered November 19, 1863, which reminded the world that the Civil War involved a larger issue of freedom and a united government based on ideals "of the people, by the people, and for the people." Upon his re-election in 1864, when the war ended and plans for peace were beginning, his Second Inaugural Address (now inscribed on the Lincoln Memorial in Washington, D.C.) showed the spirit that guided him, "With malice toward none; with charity for all; with firmness in the right... let us strive on to finish the work we are in; to bind up the nation's wounds..."

President Lincoln was assassinated at Ford's Theatre in Washington on Good Friday, April 14, 1865, by John Wilkes Booth, an actor who thought he was helping the South.

More Information About Abraham Lincoln

Born and Lived	Kentucky, Indiana
State Represented	Illinois
Party Affiliation	Republican
Siblings	Second of Six
School(s) Attended	Studied at home and while at work
Occupation(s)	Store clerk, Rail-splitter, Lawyer
Hobbies	Reading, Walking, Wrestling, Public Speaking
Political Particulars	Nicknamed "Honest Abe" Civil War, Emancipation Proclamation, Gettysburg Address
States in Union During Teenage Years	Twenty-four

ANDREW JOHNSON

Seventeenth President of the United States
Lived: 1808 – 1875   Served: 1865 – 1869

Andrew Johnson holds the unique distinction in American history to have been the only president who never went to school. He was also the first president to be impeached (accused) of "high crimes and misdemeanors." He was acquitted by only one vote in the United States Senate.

Andrew, the youngest of three children, was born in a one-room shack in Raleigh, North Carolina. His parents were poor servants who were illiterate and utterly lacking in family connections. His father was a handyman at the local inn and a janitor at the bank. He was also a sexton at the church – someone who takes care of church property, rings the bell for services and helps dig graves. When Andrew was three, his father died while rescuing a friend from drowning. This left his mother to support her two sons (the oldest daughter died at birth) by herself as best she could. She barely managed with the money she earned by weaving and spinning. A few years later she remarried, but her new husband made even less money than she did. There was little time for anything but work, and certainly none for school.

When Andrew was fourteen, his mother bound him and his older brother as apprentice tailors and indentured servants to James J. Selby. In return for their work, he provided them with food and clothing, and taught them the tailoring trade. They were supposed to serve as apprentices for six years. However, after two years the Johnson brothers ran away and broke their contract. They left because Andrew had broken a window as a prank and feared being arrested.

Mr. Selby ran an ad in the Raleigh Gazette which read, "Ran Away From the Subscriber, two apprentice boys, legally bound, named William and Andrew Johnson... I will pay the above reward [$10] to any person who will deliver said apprentices to me in Raleigh, or I will give the above reward for Andrew Johnson alone."

Andrew never had the opportunity to attend school, but he enjoyed learning and had his first real contact with books when he was an apprentice at age fourteen. Tailors often employed someone to read to the workmen as they sat at their tables stitching clothes, and this enabled Andrew to become familiar with the U.S. Constitution, American history and politics as he heard readings of the local newspaper and a few books. Johnson, once exposed, hungered for more education and began trying to teach himself to read.

While Andrew was an apprentice tailor, a Dr. Hill was hired to read aloud to him from a collection of the world's great orations. Johnson was fascinated by the stirring speeches, especially those of the English statesman William Pitt. Andrew demonstrated such an appetite for knowledge that Dr. Hill gave him the book as a gift, and he painstakingly leafed through its pages late into the night.

After fleeing from his hometown, Andrew took refuge in South Carolina, where he earned money tailoring. When he found out that his family was still living in poverty, he returned to North Carolina and took his mother, stepfather and older brother to Tennessee with him. After several months of wandering, they settled in Greeneville where, for the first time in his life, he found himself among equals. The independent mountain people worked with their hands and performed their tasks as cobblers, farmers and bricklayers with dignity. Upon hearing that the town tailor was retiring, the seventeen-year-old Andrew Johnson opened his own shop under the sign, A. JOHNSON, TAILOR.

In 1827, at the age of eighteen, Andrew met Eliza McCardle, the sixteen-year-old daughter of a Scottish shoemaker. He did the best thing in his life when he married this well-educated and well-read young girl. Although the couple was poor, they both wanted more out of life.

Andrew's wife was a very bright and ambitious girl, and she decided to teach her husband. In the evenings she became an earnest teacher, and he was an eager student. Determined that her husband should amount to something, she encouraged him to continue educating himself. She also hired a man to read to Andrew as he worked and to teach him to write. He had a very good memory and held on to all that he read and heard.

In addition to studying at home with his wife, Andrew broadened his knowledge through outside contacts. To train himself in public speaking he walked five miles several times a week to take part in debates held by the students of two nearby colleges. That is as close to a school as he ever got.

At the age of twenty Andrew accidentally began his career in politics. His friends entered his name as a candidate for alderman and he ended up winning a place on the town council, where he remained for three terms before becoming mayor. He went on to become a member of the Tennessee House of Representatives, a Tennessee State Senator, a U.S. Representative, the Governor of Tennessee, a U.S. Senator, Military Governor of Tennessee during the Civil War, and vice president during Lincoln's second term.

He became the seventeenth President of the United States when Abraham Lincoln was assassinated in 1865. Ten years after he retired Johnson became the first former president to serve in the U.S. Senate.

He did very well for a kid who didn't learn to read until he was sixteen-years-old, married at eighteen and had four children by the time he was twenty-six.

More Information About Andrew Johnson	
Born and Lived	North Carolina
State Represented	Tennessee
Party Affiliation	Democrat
Siblings	Third of Three Children
School(s) Attended	Studied at home and while at work
Occupation(s)	Tailor
Hobbies	Public Speaking, Checkers
Pet(s)	Mice
Political Particulars	Impeached in 1868 by Radical Republicans
States in Union During Teenage Years	Twenty-four

ULYSSES SIMPSON GRANT

Eighteenth President of the United States
Lived: 1822 – 1885   Served: 1869 – 1877

Ulysses S. Grant is probably best remembered as the general who commanded the Union forces to victory in the American Civil War. He is actually less well known for being the eighteenth President of the United States, even though he served two full terms. Many historians have ranked him as one of the worst presidents this nation has ever had.

Ulysses, the oldest of three boys and three girls, was born in Point Pleasant, Ohio. His father owned a tannery and a farm that was amassing a small fortune. His father was quarrelsome and boastful, the very opposite of his shy and sensitive son. It was his mother who was shy and deeply religious. His parents never scolded him or made him do anything he disliked; they simply made very clear that they loved him. Ulysses grew up in an atmosphere of neatness and self-restraint. Mrs. Grant was reputed to keep her home in immaculate order and his father's home library, with thirty-five books, was considered a marvel. The Grant home banned alcohol, swearing, blasphemy, gambling, whippings and dancing!

While other boys his age expressed themselves by being competitive and aggressive, Ulysses went his own way, managing to avoid fights and rarely getting involved in disputes or rivalries. He was withdrawn and cautious. Ulysses rarely hunted with the other boys, and when he did he simply refused to kill anything.

Horses were Ulysses' greatest interest. He was never intimidated by their size or frightened by their unpredictable movements. He was allowed to ride the workhorses twice a day and take them down to the creek for water. By age five he could be seen standing on the backs of the horses, holding the reins and balancing like a circus performer. From an early age he demonstrated a talent for handling horses, and assumed all the chores requiring their use. He cleared and plowed fields, brought in the harvests, and transported passengers for a fee. At age eight he was earning money hauling wood with a horse and cart.

By the time he was nine Ulysses had learned to ride so well that local farmers called on him to "break" their new horses or teach them to pace. He would jump astride a bucking colt and ride through the village or fields until the horse tired and became tame. He was so good that his father permitted him to buy his own horse.

The one chore Ulysses avoided whenever possible was working in his father's tannery, because the blood-caked hides nauseated him. His two brothers had no problem working in the tannery, but Ulysses preferred working on the farm. Ulysses was honest and trustworthy, and remained so all his life, so his father often sent him on business trips.

Ulysses' father learned from his own haphazard upbringing that reading was the straightest road to knowledge and success. Jesse Grant was largely self-taught, and he was determined to give his eldest son the advantages he had lacked, to enable him to succeed through education. There were no free schools at that time, so Ulysses' parents paid a small fee for him to attend classes in a one-room schoolhouse. Ulysses started school at age five, and in his class were students ranging in age from five to twenty. The school provided a very rudimentary education, with only basic readers and elementary mathematics books. Most of what he learned was by memorization and repetition, and his favorite subject was mental arithmetic. Ulysses was an average student whose only special talent seemed to be in arithmetic, but one of his teachers was impressed by how carefully Ulysses studied every book he got his hands on. Although he was an obedient student, he occasionally earned a beating with birch branch switches from his teacher.

He was by far the most intellectually able student at the little school, but the other children misread his long thoughtful and shy silences as a sign that he was mentally slow and they nicknamed him "Useless." Ulysses attended school only thirteen weeks a year, during the winter months when the farm made fewer demands. The rest of the time his education was in the hands of his parents, and it was his father who taught his oldest son to read. By age six Ulysses was able to read books written for adults.

Ulysses attended school in Georgetown until he was fourteen, when a pair of teachers sent him to another school in Kentucky. Unfortunately he grew bored there because he already knew what they were teaching. When Ulysses was fifteen, his father sent him to a private boarding academy that he attended for two years. Ulysses claimed not to be an avid reader, but in all likelihood he was the most well-read boy in town. Ulysses had a keen curiosity, but grew bored easily.

As he got older, Ulysses seemed more and more to take on the shyness of his mother. He became more sensitive to his father's boastful talk around town, because his father made it known, almost from the time Ulysses was born, that his son was a genius. His father was a co-founder of the Georgetown Debating Society and hoped his son would follow in his footsteps. But Ulysses hated arguments and detested any form of public speaking. His ambition was to be a farmer or a down-the-river trader.

Ulysses' father was very disappointed that his eldest son did not want to be part of his lucrative tannery business. Then he learned that a neighbor's son had been dismissed from the U.S. Military Academy, and he asked the congressman to appoint Ulysses to take the boy's place. He pushed his son to attend West Point, and at first Ulysses rebelled. He hated the idea of a uniform and military discipline, and the last thing he wanted to be was a soldier.

When Grant entered West Point in 1839, he was, at seventeen, the shortest and slightest cadet in his freshman class. He was all of five feet, one inch tall, and weighed only one hundred and seventeen pounds. By the time he graduated he was up to five feet, seven inches tall. Unlike the many cadets who found the first year torturous, Ulysses merely complained that it was "wearisome and uninteresting." He was an average student, but he excelled in horsemanship. Academically he did not do well, not because he wasn't intelligent, but because he did not care about grades. He did just enough to get by and not get expelled. His grades were helped or hindered by a system of merits and demerits, and Grant received numerous demerits for slovenly dress and tardiness. His classmates remembered him as lazy in his studies and careless in drill, but many also recalled quick perception and common sense. Not one for dancing or social etiquette, Ulysses preferred going to a local pub for off-limits drinking. Ulysses disliked military life and had no intention of making the army his career. "A military life," he said candidly, "had no charms for me, and I had not the faintest idea of staying in the army even if I should be graduated, which I did not expect."

Promoted to sergeant in his third year, he confessed that the higher rank was "too much" for him, and he willingly served his senior year as a private. Ulysses graduated in the middle of his class, twenty-first out of thirty-nine, but in subjects that really counted he was always in the top third of his class. His strongest subject was mathematics, and he said in his memoirs that he would have liked to have been a math professor at West Point.

After graduating from the military academy at West Point at the age of twenty-one, Grant fought in the Mexican War under General Zachary Taylor. He was a daring young officer and his men followed willingly wherever he led.

After spending eight years in the army and rising to the rank of captain, Ulysses was asked to resign because of his drinking habits and insubordination. For the next four years he attempted to be a farmer and failed. He went to work for his brothers in the tannery business as a clerk, and he remained there for a couple of years. Then the Civil War began and suddenly experienced officers were in short supply. Grant was given a job that no one else would take; he had to make a disciplined fighting unit out of a rebellious Illinois volunteer regiment that no one had been able to tame. He whipped it into shape and was promoted to brigadier general. Throughout his career, Grant would be both praised and criticized for his willingness to fight even when it cost a disproportionate number of his soldiers' lives. He was given the nickname "the Butcher."

He was also criticized for his drinking. When someone complained to President Lincoln that General Grant was a drunk, Lincoln's reply was, "Tell me what he drinks so I can have all my other generals do the same." "I cannot spare this man," Lincoln said, "he fights!" It has never been proven that Grant was ever inebriated while in battle.

General Grant trapped the main Confederate army south of Richmond and forced a surrender in April, 1865, ending the bloody Civil War. At that point, he was the most revered man in the Union. His war-hero status led to his election as the eighteenth President of the United States.

More Information About Ulysses S. Grant

Born	Ohio
State Represented	Illinois
Party Affiliation	Republican
Siblings	First of Six Children
School(s) Attended	West Point
Occupation(s)	Army Officer
Hobbies	Horseback Riding, Swimming, Drawing and Painting
Political Particulars	Civil War General-in-Chief
States in Union During Teenage Years	Thirty-six

RUTHERFORD BIRCHARD HAYES

Nineteenth President of the United States
Lived: 1822 – 1893   Served: 1877 – 1881

It was during Rutherford Hayes' administration that this country had its first electric lights and its first telephone.

Rutherford was born in Delaware, Ohio, and he was the oldest of five children, although only he and one sister lived into adulthood. Hayes' father, a successful store and orchard owner, died two months before Rutherford was born.

For the first two years of his life Rutherford's mother worried about his survival. He was weak, and the deaths of two of her earlier children terrified her. Living in the depths of almost unbearable grief his mother seemed to find strength in taking care of her baby. She dedicated herself to him, sheltering the boy from harm and showering him with motherly affection and attention. Until he was seven he was not allowed to play with children outside his family, and he was nine before he could take part in sports. He just stayed home, where he had the love of his mother and his relatives.

His mother was a strict Presbyterian who loved to talk about religion and politics. She engaged wandering ministers in long discussions of the latest ideas about God and Christianity. The family often talked about problems concerning government, slavery, and politics in Washington.

With no father, young Hayes sought fathering from his bachelor uncle who became the children's guardian. Rutherford looked mainly to him, a self-educated, hard-drinking frontiersman, for love and affection. Rutherford wanted to be just like his uncle, and he became Rutherford's lifelong mentor.

Rutherford also admired his older sister, who was a precocious child and his constant companion. He looked up to her as his "protector and nurse," and he would later call her his inspiration. She, even more than his uncle or mother, urged Rutherford to work to become "somebody important." She believed in him and identified with him, and she shared his dreams so much that he grew up anxious to fulfill her expectations.

Rutherford stood out from other boys his age because of his big dreams, his self-confidence, and his steadfastness. He was a stout, happy child, with a great personality and many friends who gave him the nickname "Ruddy." As a child, he kept a diary that he wrote in throughout his life. He was always ambitious, dreaming of future glory by performing some virtuous or patriotic act, and envisioning achieving military fame. Many men in his family had been soldiers, some of whom had fought in the American Revolution and the War of 1812.

Rutherford loved to play orator, and one cousin was so impressed with his cleverness that she was sure he would one day become President of the United States. He said of himself that he was "remarkable for self-esteem," but he also confessed at times to be "nervous to the verge of disaster." He "went to pieces on the slightest provocation." Rutherford ascribed his nervousness to a fear of insanity in his family. Both his mother and sister had bouts of severe depression.

Hayes learned the fundamentals of reading, writing, and arithmetic from a harsh schoolmaster in Delaware, Ohio. He was a champion speller and he later boasted, "Not one in a thousand could spell me down." At age fourteen he attended the Norwalk Academy, a Methodist school in Ohio. The next year he entered a college preparatory academy in Connecticut where the schoolmaster wrote in a progress report, "Rutherford is industrious, well-informed, polite, and respected by his peers."

At age sixteen Hayes enrolled in Kenyon College in Gambier, Ohio. He was a good student, taking a special interest in philosophy and debate, but detesting science. He studied Greek and Latin classics, Christian ethics, theology, and other subjects considered necessary for a cultured and educated man of his time. His early love for oratory stayed with him at Kenyon, where he participated in debating tournaments that involved the issue of slavery. As a young man, he did not have strong feelings about the subject, yet he later fought to abolish slavery. His uncle and mother frowned upon slavery on moral grounds, but like many northerners, they strongly opposed the abolitionists. Abolitionists, they believed, threatened the harmony of North and South and went against the Constitution, which left the issue of slavery up to the individual states.

Although there was rigid discipline at the college, Rutherford did indulge in some forbidden fun... he loved to go hunting. He also resisted his teacher's efforts to win his declaration of faith in Christianity. "There are now but ten in the whole college who are not changed," he wrote to his mother – a sure sign of his independent thinking.

His mother was not pleased to hear this. She was already upset, when, on returning home one vacation, Rutherford used a vulgar phrase he had picked up at college. "I never heard you say, 'By George,' til the last time you were home, nor speak any other such language!" she remarked in a letter.

At age nineteen Rutherford wrote in his diary that he was "determined from henceforth to use what means I have to acquire a character distinguished for energy, firmness and perseverance." He graduated as class valedictorian in 1842 at the age of twenty. After pondering several careers, he decided to study law, and upon his graduation from Kenyon he entered Harvard Law School.

After finishing law school in 1845, he spent the next seventeen years practicing law. At the beginning of the Civil War, Hayes was a successful thirty-nine-year-old practicing attorney in Cincinnati, Ohio. Because of his love of the Union and his fighting spirit, he volunteered to join the army. The war brought out qualities that Rutherford had never before discovered in himself. During the four years he served so bravely, he rose from captain to major general. In 1864, while the war still raged, his friends nominated him for a seat in Congress. He refused to campaign, stating resolutely, "an officer fit for duty who at this crisis would abandon his post to electioneer ought to be scalped." His friends, including author Mark Twain, campaigned for him, and he won the election by a large majority. He refused to be seated as a congressman until the war was over, and only then did he resign from the army.

After two terms as a congressman, he went on to become a two-term Governor of Ohio. Then, in 1876, Rutherford Hayes took part in the most controversial presidential election in American history. Samuel Tilden, a Democrat, won the popular vote by 300,000 votes, and the electoral vote was 203 for Tilden and 166 for Hayes. Rutherford Hayes went to bed that night believing he had lost the election. However, the Republicans claimed that three states had not allowed the Negroes to vote, and without the electoral votes from those states the Republicans would have won by one electoral vote. Congress decided to set up a special fifteen-member electoral commission (with eight Republicans and seven Democrats) to decide the election. The deciding vote was eight to seven in favor of Hayes, and he became the nineteenth President of the United States.

More Information About Rutherford B. Hayes	
State Represented	Ohio
Party Affiliation	Republican
Siblings	First of Five Children
School(s) Attended	Kenyon College, Harvard Law School
Occupation(s)	Lawyer
Hobbies	Croquet, Hunting, Public Speaking, Spelling
Political Particulars	Helped restore dignity and integrity to executive office; Nicknamed "Dark Horse President" because of controversial election
States in Union During Teenage Years	Twenty-six

JAMES ABRAM GARFIELD

Twentieth President of the United States
Lived: 1831 – 1881   Served: March, 1881 – July, 1881

James Garfield was the first President of the United States who was left-handed. He had the unique ability to write Greek with his left hand while at the same time writing Latin with his right hand. He was also the second president to be assassinated while in office (the first was Abraham Lincoln in 1865).

James, the youngest of five children, was born in Orange, Ohio. He was the last president to be born in a crude, one-room log cabin. He grew up in poverty on his father's farm, and he knew he would have to work for everything he got. Still, the poverty of the frontier was quite different from that of the city – neighbors often shared the burden of earning a living from the land.

James was a year-and-a-half old when his father died of a throat infection while fighting a fire. His father was only thirty-three-years-old and was known everywhere as a champion wrestler.

"At almost every turning point in my life," he wrote of his mother, "she has been the molding agent." After the death of her husband at such a young age, Mrs. Garfield struggled to keep the family and the farm together. She was the first mother of a United States President to attend her son's inauguration, and she lived at the White House during his short time in office.

When James was three-years-old, his sister began carrying him almost six miles through the woods to and from the little red schoolhouse they attended. Their mother decided that the township should have a school of its own, so she offered a corner of her land for it. The neighbors helped build a crude log schoolhouse, and James was able to go to school and still be close enough to help with the farm chores.

By the time he was ten-years-old James had learned to do almost everything around the farm. He not only helped the other children and his mother at home, but when they had finished their work he frequently went to other farms and worked for the neighbors so he might make some extra money to help his mother. James had very little time to play, because all spring and summer the children worked, and during the winter they went to the little neighborhood school.

Before he was four-years-old James had learned to read, and he loved reading the family bible. By the time he was ten he had borrowed and read nearly all the books in his neighborhood, and from then on he was an avid reader and a great student. When James read, a whole new world opened up to him, in which his imagination could carry him far beyond the little cabin in the woods. He could share in the adventures of exciting heroes and great men, and he could study new ideas and stretch his mind. He devoured the few books in the family library, and read them again and again until he knew almost every page by heart.

He loved books more than most boys, or even most men of his time. He developed a hunger for knowledge that lasted throughout his life. This was his strength – his willingness to open his mind allowed him to search for all the information he could get about anything that interested him.

James had a quick mind, and was curious about everything. His mother tried as best she could to answer his constant questions. She was determined to give James a good education so that he might someday become a teacher, or attain an even higher post as a preacher.

There were no history lessons in school, but he found a history book and taught himself from that. He and a cousin read *Robinson Crusoe* by Daniel Defoe, and his mind was filled with the adventures from the desert island. When he discovered a book of pirate stories, he poured over it until the pages wore thin. That was the life he wanted. Not the monotony of farm chores, of school, clearing a field, or any of the dull and boring things he knew too well. Instead he longed for a life of freedom and great adventure. The tales absorbed his mind until they became more real to him than anything on the farm.

James' older brother laughed at him for his romantic notions and his mother was sometimes annoyed, especially when he neglected his work to read or play. She was bothered, too, when he began to get into trouble at school.

When James was thirteen, he began to work for wages during vacation times, partly because they needed any money he could bring home, and partly for the satisfaction of earning on his own. Still, the kind of work was much the same — for twenty-five cents a day he chopped wood, planted corn, cradled wheat, or mowed hay. Although he was eager to help his mother, he was anything but an enthusiastic farmer. There was a big difference between the two Garfield brothers. Thomas was quiet, easy-going, and wanted nothing more than a farmer's life. James was enterprising, ambitious and had a temperament that drove him to seek new experiences and repeatedly test himself.

At seventeen, inspired by all his adventure stories, James left home with the romantic idea of becoming a sailor on the Great Lakes, but he gave up that notion when a ship's captain cursed him and drove him away. A cousin then hired him to drive a team of horses and tow a barge along the Ohio Canal. During his six weeks on the canal he fell overboard fourteen times, a dangerous habit considering he never learned how to swim. On one occasion he got terribly ill with malaria and almost died. He still dreamed of one day becoming a sailor, but his mother convinced him to continue his education.

Most of Garfield's education until he went to an academy at age seventeen was informal. At the academy his studies included algebra, English grammar, Latin and Greek, botany and geography. He worked his way through school doing carpentry, and at the age of twenty he enrolled at the Eclectic Institute in Hiram, Ohio. It was here that Garfield discovered he had the power to sway an audience — he was a natural speaker. In order to pay for this school, he worked as a janitor.

At age twenty-three James entered Williams College in Williamstown, Massachusetts as a junior, where he finally blossomed intellectually. As the oldest student on campus, he was respected and admired. He was the school's debate champion and was active in a variety of extracurricular activities, including serving as president of both the Philogian (literary) society and the Mills theological society, as editor of the Williams quarterly, and as a member of the Equitable Fraternity. He graduated with honors in 1856 at age twenty-five.

After graduation James considered taking up the ministry, because he was already an accomplished preacher, but he decided to teach instead. He returned to Hiram College as a professor of ancient languages and literature. The following year, at the age of twenty-six he was chosen as president of the college.

While serving as president of the college, James' ambition drove him forward, and he decided to study law on his own. He was admitted to the Ohio bar in 1860.

A year later the Civil War began and Garfield volunteered. He was immediately commissioned as a lieutenant colonel, and in the next two years he rose to the rank of major general. In 1862 he was elected to Congress and resigned his commission in the army. He was re-elected nine times and remained in Congress for the next eighteen years.

In 1880, at age forty-nine, at the Republican National Convention, James Garfield won the nomination for president on the thirty-sixth ballot. A mere one hundred days after Garfield was inaugurated he was struck by an assassin's bullet, and he died two months later.

More Information About James A. Garfield

State Represented	Ohio
Party Affiliation	Republican
Siblings	Fifth of Five Children
School(s) Attended	Williams College
Occupation(s)	Teacher, Preacher, Lawyer
Hobbies	Billiards, Reading, Debating
Political Particulars	He was assassinated after being in office for only six months
States in Union During Teenage Years	Thirty-one

CHESTER ALAN ARTHUR

Twenty-first President of the United States
Lived: 1829 – 1886   Served: 1881 – 1885

Chester Arthur is said to be the most unknown of our nation's presidents to date (he is remembered as one of the four "lost presidents" who served rather uneventfully after the Civil War: Hayes, Garfield, Arthur, and B. Harrison). It is unlikely that he would ever have become president had President Garfield not been assassinated; he was never elected to public office before he was nominated as vice president. His contemporaries knew him as the "elegant" president because of the way he dressed – it is said that he had eighty pairs of trousers and changed his clothes many times a day while in office.

Chester, the fifth child and first son in a family of six girls and three boys, was born in Fairfield, Vermont. His father had come to America from Northern Ireland and worked as a teacher and a Baptist minister. Like many rural ministers, Chester's father seldom stayed long in any one post. He lived in relative poverty, since country ministers got very little to live on in those days. We know little of Chester's mother except that she grew up on her father's farm.

During the first nine years of his life, Chester moved with his family five times, settling at last in Union Village, New York, where he attended a local school. Even with all his moving around, Chester was a happy child – bright, active, impulsive, and given to boyish pranks.

A schoolmate recalled that Chester showed leadership skills at an early age: "When Chester was a boy, you might see him in the village street after a [rain] shower, watching boys building a mud dam across the rivulet (a small stream) in the roadway. Pretty soon he would be ordering this one to bring stones, another sticks, and others sod and mud to finish the dam."

Chester was not afraid to work, and now and then he earned some money by helping on farms or doing other odd jobs. He liked reading and studying, and loved playing sports. He learned a lot from his father and from books.

When he was fourteen-years-old, he went to Union College in New York, where he joined one of the social fraternities. He sought wild adventures and loved adding a hint of danger. He was a leader in pulling pranks in college, one of which involved dumping the school bell in the Erie Canal. He was fond of parades and processions, of class games and fun, and was a jovial, active, and sociable guy.

He studied a little, but amused himself more. He gave his books only what time he could spare from his sports. Nevertheless, he was an excellent student, and he was one of six in his class of one hundred admitted to the national honor society Phi Beta Kappa.

He taught school to help pay his way through college, and he kept at it for two more years, saving what he could until he had a few hundred dollars. While he was teaching, he studied law, which he was able to continue in New York City with the money he had saved. He was looking for more profitable employment than teaching country boys how to read, write, and do arithmetic.

Young Arthur did not lack ambition. His purpose was to rise in the world, and he wanted to attain fame and fortune quickly. It seemed to him that the great and growing west was the place to do this, so after a period of practice in New York, he and another young lawyer set out to try their luck. They traveled around the west seeking their fortune, but they didn't find it waiting for them. They discovered they would have to work just as hard out there as they did in New York, perhaps even harder. So they turned back and became partners in New York. For ten years Arthur kept up his law practice, at first in partnership and then by himself.

Chester successfully represented a Negro woman in her lawsuit against a Brooklyn streetcar company for forcibly ejecting her from a Whites-only car. This was a landmark case that helped promote the desegregation of public transportation in New York City.

During the Civil War, Arthur served in the army as quartermaster general of the state of New York, and he was later appointed by President Grant as Collector of the Port of New York.

In 1881, after being vice president for only two months, Chester Arthur became president after President Garfield was assassinated.

One reason we know so little about Chester Arthur is that he had all his public and private papers in his possession burned just before he died.

More Information About Chester A. Arthur	
Born	Vermont
State Represented	New York
Party Affiliation	Republican
Siblings	Fifth of Nine Children
School(s) Attended	Union College
Occupation(s)	Teacher, Lawyer, Inspector General
Hobbies	Sports
Political Particulars In Office	Pendleton Act (established bipartisan Civil Service Commission), Chinese Exclusion Act of 1882 (first general federal immigration law)
States in Union During Teenage Years	Thirty

GROVER CLEVELAND

22nd and 24th President of the United States
Lived: 1837 – 1908   Served: 1885 – 1889; 1893 – 1897

Stephen Grover Cleveland was forty-nine-years-old when he married twenty-one-year-old Frances Folsom, and was the only president to get married while in the White House. He was the eighth president never to attend college, and he is the only president to have served two terms not in succession.

Grover, the fifth child in a family of four brothers and five sisters, was born in Caldwell, New Jersey. His father was a village clergyman and a relative of Moses Cleveland, the founder of Cleveland, Ohio. He had very little to live on, and it took the help of his sons to survive. Grover's mother was the daughter of a prosperous law book publisher, and she was very much involved in making sure that all of her children got a good education.

When Grover was four, the family moved to Fayetteville, New York. Grover's father was very strict regarding his children's attendance at church. It was not a time for merriment and fun, but rather an opportunity for solitude and reflection. For Grover every Sunday was torture, and it was on one such Sunday that the boy received an invitation he could not refuse:

> "We're going to ring the schoolhouse bell at midnight," a friend told Grover. "Do you wanna come?"
> Grover's face brightened with just the thought of such a daring deed. "You bet I do!"

All their plans to get into the schoolhouse worked perfectly. Promptly at midnight the loud bell tolled, and the men and women of

Fayetteville scrambled into their clothes and ran from their homes to see what was happening. Sadly, the three young bell-ringers had planned everything except their escape. Somehow they managed to lock themselves inside the schoolhouse, only to be brought out and escorted home by their disgruntled parents.

The family of a country minister led a hard life. The Cleveland family had little money and moved several times. Grover took time out from his chores of chopping wood, growing a garden, and baby-sitting for his younger siblings, to fish in the nearby lake or take a dip in the creek. Still he learned early the value of using his time wisely. In an essay written when he was nine, Grover declared, "If we expect to become great and good men, and be respected and esteemed by our friends, we must improve our time when we are young."

Grover's father was a graduate of Yale University, and although a minister's salary did not go far in raising nine children, it was always understood that the Cleveland sons would receive the best formal education possible. Having learned the basics at home from his parents, Grover, at age eleven, was enrolled in a local private academy with a college-preparatory curriculum. He must have been a good student, because he got into the high school when he was several years younger than the other boys; his goal was to be at the head of his class.

In 1850 Grover's father received a better position that forced him and his family to move again. For a brief time Grover attended Clinton Academy, until the family encountered financial difficulties. To earn spare cash Cleveland picked up odd jobs around the Erie Canal, and at age fifteen he left his family in Clinton to work as a clerk in John McVicar's store in Fayetteville for $50 a year plus room and board.

It was not an easy life for a fifteen-year-old boy. Separated from the rest of his family, Grover shared a room above the store with another boy. Each slept in a rope bed covered with a straw mattress. The boys rose before six each morning, washed outside in the village store trough, then swept and straightened the store before they opened at seven o'clock. During the day they waited on customers, ran errands, made deliveries, and unloaded merchandise; they ate their meals whenever they could find time.

This routine quickly grew monotonous, and Grover felt that he needed to find something else to keep his mind active. While at Clinton Academy, he had enjoyed studying about ancient Greek and Roman philosophers and orators. Grover decided to organize a debating group consisting of Fayetteville boys, and they met at the general store each week. They talked about current events around the country, argued their ideas, and discussed the government. Carefully Grover set aside his salary, eagerly planning to attend Hamilton College in Clinton the first chance he could.

When Grover was sixteen his father died, leaving his mother with four small children to care for. Grover faced an important decision, to either continue with his plans for college or return home and help his mother. Family responsibility won out, and the money he had set aside for college was added to the family's funds.

Grover's older brother arranged for his appointment as an assistant teacher in the literary department of the New York Institute for the Blind where he taught reading, writing, arithmetic, and geography. He disliked the job and quit after one year to join the rest of his family in Holland Patent, New York. Although he longed to continue his education, he turned down an offer from a benefactor to send him to college if he would enter the ministry upon graduation.

He began looking for full-time employment, but his lack of a college education prevented him from obtaining the positions he wanted. "Go back to school," friends advised him, "you need that education."

When Grover was seventeen, he decided to go out west and see if he could make his way in the world, but he only got as far as Buffalo. He had an uncle who lived on a nearby farm and was writing a book. He asked Grover to stop and help him on the farm, but what the boy really wanted to do was study law. Some of his favorite experiences had been with the debating group in Fayetteville, and a college education was not required to become a lawyer. After some time on the farm he got a chance to become a clerk in a lawyer's office in Buffalo, and he spent all his spare time reading law books.

He still lived with his uncle two miles away, and every day, rain or shine, Grover walked to and from the office. It was not too much for a strong boy like him; and he had to live very cheaply, since he was only paid four dollars a week for his work.

At age nineteen, Grover began to work as a clerk in the law office of Rogers, Bowen, and Rogers. The serious, quiet Cleveland worked hard for four dollars a week, which paid for his room and board at the home of a fellow law clerk. He studied hard, and at the age of twenty-two he was admitted to the bar.

Grover Cleveland

Grover was drafted during the Civil War but chose to purchase a substitute – a legal option under the terms of the Conscription Act of 1863 that allowed someone else to serve in his place. He paid $150 for George Brinski, a thirty-two-year-old Polish immigrant, to enter the Union army in his place.

Grover Cleveland went on to become a sheriff, mayor of Buffalo, and Governor of New York, before winning the presidential election of 1884. He lost the 1888 election to Benjamin Harrison, but he was elected President of the United States again in 1892.

More Information About Grover Cleveland	
Born	New Jersey
State Represented	New York
Party Affiliation	Democrat
Siblings	Fifth of Nine Children
School(s) Attended	High School at Clinton Academy, Did not attend college
Occupation(s)	Store clerk, Teacher, Lawyer
Hobbies	Fishing, Swimming
Political Particulars in Office	Nicknamed "Guardian President" because he used the presidential veto often to balance power in the executive and legislative branches; dealt with an economic Depression and a railroad strike
States in Union During Teenage Years	Thirty-one

BENJAMIN HARRISON

Twenty-third President of the United States
Lived: 1833 – 1901   Served: 1889 – 1893

John Scott Harrison, a farmer and two-term U.S. Congressman, is the only man whose father, William Henry Harrison, and son, Benjamin Harrison, were both Presidents of the United States. Benjamin Harrison was named after his great-grandfather, who was one of the signers of the Declaration of Independence and a Governor of Virginia. Benjamin was seven-years-old when his grandfather became the ninth President of the United States. Benjamin was five feet, six inches tall, the second shortest president (next to James Madison) and the shortest general during the Civil War.

Benjamin was born on his grandfather's farm in North Bend, Ohio. He was the fifth of his father's thirteen children, the second of ten children from a second marriage. His mother was of Scottish background, was a strict Presbyterian, and distrusted cucumbers. She once wrote to him, "I hope you will be prudent in your diet and abstain from cucumbers." She died when Benjamin was seventeen, while giving birth to her tenth child at the age of forty.

Benjamin was short and stocky, and he grew up like any farm boy in the new states that had been created from the Northwest Territory shortly before his birth. He helped on his father's farm, some 400 acres on the banks of the Ohio River, near the mouth of the Big Miami River. He helped his father feed the livestock, plant corn, gather hay, water the vegetable garden, milk cows, and many other tasks. Days began as soon as the sun came up and ended after sunset.

It was not an easy life, and it got worse for Benjamin's parents over the years. In addition to the deaths of three of their children, they had to cope with a great deal of illness in the rest of the family. Colds, influenza, scarlet fever and lung infections seemed to plague the Harrison household year after year. The cost of doctor's visits and medicines led to severe money shortages. Although the early 19th century was a time of large families, it was also a time of disease, hardship, primitive medical treatments, and frequent family sorrows.

Because the family lived too far from any town for the children to attend regular schools, Benjamin's father built a one-room log schoolhouse on his farm and hired private tutors each winter to teach his children reading, writing, and arithmetic. One of those tutors, Harriet Root, said that Benjamin was the "brightest of the family." She also said that he was "terribly stubborn about many things." (This seems to be a common characteristic among many presidents!)

When Benjamin was fourteen, he was sent to a college preparatory school called Farmers College. His father wanted him to become a doctor. He learned Latin, Greek, mathematics, and philosophy, and he developed a lifelong interest in history, politics and sociology. He also delighted in the library books he found at the college. He loved Dickens, Thackeray, and all the modern classics, and he occasionally read the tales of Washington Irving.

Often in later years Harrison said how grateful he was to have had such a good and inspiring teacher. Upon leaving Farmers College he wrote his thanks to his favorite teacher, "Having for some years enjoyed the benefit of your instruction, and being now about to pass from under your care, I would be truly ungrateful were I not to return my warmest thanks for the lively interest you have ever maintained in my welfare and advancement in religious as well as scientific knowledge."

Although a good student, Benjamin didn't like the idea of constant study. He kept hearing reports of Indian attacks in the Northwest Territory and he longed to do what he could to combat the savage forces.

Benjamin also liked to have a good time. According to his biographer Lew Wallace, Benjamin as a boy spent much leisure time playing games such as "snowballing, town-ball, bull-pen, shinny and baste." He loved sports and played with spirit and guts, even though he was shorter than most. He also became an avid fisherman and an expert shot.

Presidents Were Teenagers Too

Benjamin had another source of education during his childhood in his grandfather's large library. As soon as Benjamin showed his intelligence and his love of learning, he was given permission to read from General William Henry Harrison's collection. It included many volumes on American history that Benjamin found very exciting.

At age sixteen he came up with this incredible insight: "The manner by which women are treated is good criterion to judge the true state of society. If we knew but this one feature in a character of a nation, we may easily judge the rest, for as society advances, the true character of women is discovered."

Benjamin held his mother in the highest esteem. "She is my refuge and strength, a very present help in time of trouble." Soon after he entered Miami University in Oxford, Ohio as a junior, he took the necessary instructions and became member of the Presbyterian Church. He realized that his mother had been a prop for him and that her strength had come from her deep religious beliefs. It was this Christian conscientiousness that led him to give far greater attention to his studies at Miami University than he did at Farmers College.

After only two years, and not yet eighteen-years-old, Benjamin graduated from Miami University. He liked history and political science; he took special interest in any study that led him to consider questions of social or political life. He ranked fourth in his class of sixteen boys, and he distinguished himself as a skilled debater.

Benjamin early exhibited the qualities of a good orator. He had a strong voice, clear diction, and he spoke easily and well on any subject that interested him. When he became a member of the Union Literary Society, he took full advantage of every opportunity to do public speaking and take part in debates.

While Benjamin was at Miami University, his long-time girlfriend Caroline Scott was a student at the Oxford Female Institute, a school founded by her father. During the two years that Benjamin was at the university, he spent so many evenings with her that he became known on campus as "the pious moonlight dude." By the time he graduated they had secretly gotten engaged. He was seventeen and she was eighteen at the time of their engagement, but they decided to postpone the wedding so he could study law and she could finish school. In 1853, when he was nineteen and she was twenty, Benjamin and Carrie were married.

Benjamin made up his mind to be a lawyer, and he allowed his father to pull the necessary strings to get him accepted in the notable Cincinnati firm of Storer and Gwynne. Two years later he was admitted to the bar, at the age of twenty-one, then moved to Indianapolis, Indiana to begin a lucrative law practice.

Besides becoming a successful attorney, Benjamin Harrison, at age twenty-eight, volunteered to serve in the U.S. Army during the Civil War. He rose in rank from second lieutenant to brigadier general, and was respectfully referred to as "Little Ben" by those who served under him.

Twice he ran for Governor of Indiana and lost. Then at age forty-eight, he was elected by the Indiana Legislature to the U.S. Senate. After being defeated for a second term in the Senate, Benjamin Harrison was elected the twenty-third President of the United States. Interestingly enough, he lost the popular vote to Grover Cleveland, but won the electoral vote. Harrison would lose re-election to the previous president, Grover Cleveland.

More Information About Benjamin Harrison	
Born	Ohio
State Represented	Indiana
Party Affiliation	Republican
Siblings	Fifth of Thirteen Children
School(s) Attended	Miami University in Oxford, Ohio
Occupation(s)	Lawyer
Hobbies	Hunting, Reading, Debating
Pet	Goat
Political Particulars In Office	Grandfather was 9th U.S. President; Convened the first Pan-American Conference in 1889; Signed the landmark Sherman Antitrust Act
States in Union During Teenage Years	Thirty-one

WILLIAM McKINLEY

Twenty-Fifth President of the United States
Lived: 1843 – 1901   Served: 1897 – 1901

William McKinley was the third president to die as a result of an as-sassin's bullet. He was a president known to be gentle and kind.

Early in life McKinley developed a strong interest in politics and had an ambition for high office. Many years later he said, "I have never been in doubt since I was old enough to think intelligently that I would someday become president." Yet, no matter how successful William McKinley became politically, his mother was terribly disap-pointed because her boy failed to become a preacher. She feared the temptation to which he would be exposed when he was nominated for president.

William, the seventh of nine children, was born in Niles, Ohio, a rural town with a population of about three hundred. A country store occupied part of the first floor of the long, two-story family home. His parents were not rich, but they had enough to live on. His father worked so hard in the iron manufacturing business that for many years William only saw his father on Sundays.

McKinley was known as a spirited, fun-loving kid, and during the Mexican War, he and his playmates delighted in drilling like soldiers. He enjoyed outdoor sports like fishing, camping, ice skating, horse-back riding, and swimming. Once William nearly drowned, but he was rescued as he went under for the third time. When he was nine, the McKinley's moved about ten miles south to Poland, Ohio where he spent the remainder of his childhood.

William McKinley

William learned the fundamentals at a Niles, Ohio public school. In Poland he attended the local public school, and then he enrolled at the Poland Seminary, a Methodist institution. He liked school and became a keenly observant young man. He was a delicate child who studied hard and learned his lessons easily. A gifted instructor at the school influenced his life more than any other woman outside his family. His favorite subject was speech – a naturally gifted orator, he organized and served as the first president of the school's Literary and Debating Society.

At age seventeen, McKinley entered the junior class of Allegheny College in Pennsylvania. Within the year he was forced by illness (apparently physical exhaustion from studying too hard) to drop out. He had planned to resume his studies after a period of convalescence at home, but family finances suffered during the depression following the Panic of 1857, and he had to go to work. He taught for a term during 1860-1861 at the Kerr District School in Poland, and then he clerked at the town post office before taking part in the Civil War.

When the Civil War broke out in 1861, William, who was only eighteen at the time, was the first man in his hometown to volunteer as a private in the Union Army. He became a sergeant in a regiment commanded by another future president, Rutherford B. Hayes. McKinley carried food and water to the regiment during the battle of Antietam; later his bravery under fire earned him a commission as a second lieutenant. By the end of the war he had been promoted to major.

After the war, McKinley decided to become a lawyer, and he studied in the law office of County Judge Charles E. Glidden in Youngstown, Ohio. At age twenty-three William entered law school in Albany, New York but dropped out before graduation. He was admitted to the bar the following year and began practicing law in Canton, Ohio.

At age thirty-four, William McKinley was elected to the U.S. House of Representatives. He was re-elected six times and served in Congress for fourteen years before serving two terms as Governor of Ohio. He was then elected twice as President of the United States.

McKinley presided over a friendly administration in a relatively prosperous time in the nation's history. His administration was also dominated by the 100-day war, in which the United States destroyed the Spanish fleet outside Santiago harbor in Cuba and annexed the Philippines, Guam and Puerto Rico. McKinley's second term came to a tragic end in September, 1901. He was standing in a receiving line at the Buffalo Pan-American Exposition when a deranged anarchist shot him twice. He died eight days later, at the age of fifty-eight.

More Information About William McKinley	
State Represented	Ohio
Party Affiliation	Republican
Siblings	Seventh of Nine Children
School(s) Attended	Allegheny College, Albany Law School
Occupation(s)	Lawyer, Teacher
Hobbies	Fishing, Camping, Ice-Skating, Horseback Riding, Swimming, Debating
Pet	Yellow Parrot
Political Particulars in Office	100-day War; Assassinated in office
States in Union During Teenage Years	Thirty-four

THEODORE ROOSEVELT

Twenty-Sixth President of the United States
Lived: 1858 – 1919   Served: 1901 – 1909

With the assassination of President McKinley, Theodore Roosevelt, only forty-two-years-old, became the youngest president in the nation's history, and the fifth vice president to become President of the United States upon the death of a president. Theodore Roosevelt is known for quoting a favorite proverb: "Speak softly, and carry a big stick." "Teddy bears" were given their name because Roosevelt was once depicted in a cartoon sparing the life of a cub while hunting.

Theodore, the second of four children and the older of two sons, was born in New York City. He was born into a family with a long history of wealth, good works, and public service. His father was a partner in a firm that imported plate glass. His mother was born and raised on a plantation in Georgia, and until the day she died she never relinquished her sympathies to the South and the Confederates.

Theodore was a pale, sickly boy, who struggled with such severe asthma that for much of his early childhood he had to sleep propped up in bed or slouching in a chair. Despite this and frequent bouts with coughs, colds, diarrhea, and other illnesses, he was a hyperactive, often mischievous kid. He was once chased down by his father for biting his sister's arm.

While playing with friends one day, Theodore discovered that he was nearsighted. The other children easily read an advertisement on a billboard some distance away. "Not only was I unable to read the sign, but I could not even see the letters," Roosevelt wrote later, and from then on he wore glasses.

Presidents Were Teenagers Too

Theodore's father worried constantly about his son's health and lavished the tenderest care on him during his cruel asthma attacks. Yet he feared that the boy might become an invalid or allow himself to find in books a substitute, rather than a supplement, for a life of action and accomplishment.

Theodore loved both books and the outdoors, and he was able to combine these interests in his study of nature. His dresser drawers smelled of dead mice and birds, and quite often, so did Theodore. When he was seven, he saw a dead seal laid out on a slab at the local fish market, and he got excited because the seal reminded him of all the adventure stories in far-away places he had read about. He visited the fish market every day to look at the seal; he even made careful measurements of its size and wrote them down in a pocket notebook. Eventually the amused fish seller gave him the seal's head.

Determined to become a zoologist, Theodore caught countless creatures large and small, stored them all around the house, and examined and catalogued them. He established The Roosevelt Museum of Natural History in his bedroom. At age nine he wrote a precociously learned paper "The Natural History of Insects," based on his personal observations.

When he was ten, and again when he was fourteen, Theodore went with his family on yearlong trips abroad. On one trip he toured Europe, spent Christmas in Rome, Italy and kissed the hand of Pope Pius IX. When he toured Egypt, he climbed to the top of the Pyramids and visited the Holy Land in Jerusalem, before spending several months in Dresden, Germany.

When Theodore was twelve, he had the unhappy experience of being teased by four boys throughout a stagecoach ride to Maine and was unable to fight them off because he was so puny. This humiliating experience convinced Theodore that he needed to learn to defend himself. With his father's encouragement, young Roosevelt became determined to improve his body. He began a vigorous program of exercise in a gymnasium his father built on the second floor of their home.

He took boxing lessons and eventually won a lightweight contest in a championship match sponsored by his instructor. He continued with his body building exercises, and by the time he went to college he was in excellent shape. For the rest of his life Theodore tried to outdo everyone else with his energy and stamina.

Roosevelt overcame his asthma and built up unusual strength. "There were all kinds of things of which I was afraid at first," he later confessed, "but by acting as if I was not afraid I gradually ceased to be afraid." It was a triumph of will over trauma, confirming in Roosevelt a chip-on-the-shoulder arrogance that would both empower and burden him throughout his life.

Theodore's delicate health as a young child had prevented him from attending school. When his parents finally did send him to school, he became ill and left after only a month. For the rest of his childhood he studied at home. Theodore's first teacher was an aunt who taught him the basics of reading and writing. She also recounted tales of the South and the Confederacy, which gave her young student a love of history. A number of other private tutors followed. The Roosevelts even hired a teacher of taxidermy (the art of preparing, stuffing and mounting the skins of animals in lifelike forms) to encourage his affinity for natural history.

In Dresden, Germany, in the summer of 1873, at the age of fifteen, Theodore studied German and French under Fraulein Anna Minkwitz, who predicted of her pupil, "He will surely one day be a great professor, or who knows, he may become President of the United States."

Preparation for college required concentrated study after Roosevelt's spotty succession of tutors. Returning to New York later that year in 1873, he underwent intensive tutoring with Arthur Cutler to prepare for the Harvard entrance examination, which he passed at the age of seventeen. Roosevelt was a serious scholar. He excelled in the sciences, German, rhetoric and philosophy, but he didn't like studying ancient languages. In his senior year he began working on his first book, "The Naval War of 1812," a study he preferred to more classical disciplines. But his interests in naval history and natural science did not preclude other activities.

Theodore was very active at Harvard: he was librarian of the Procellian Club, secretary of the Hasty Pudding Club, vice president of the National History Club, editor of the *Advocate*, and founder of the Finance Club, and still found time to write and lecture before the Ornithological Club.

Theodore boxed and trained in the college gym. He was a runner-up for the campus lightweight boxing championship, losing the title to C.S. Hanks. Although outclassed by Hanks in a particularly bloody slugfest, Roosevelt was long remembered for his sportsmanship during the bout. At the end of one round Hanks bloodied Roosevelt's nose after the bell rang, drawing a chorus of jeers from ringside. Roosevelt turned to the crowd and called for quiet, explaining that Hanks had not heard the bell. Then he walked over to his opponent and shook his hand, to the pleasure of the fans.

At age twenty-one Theodore graduated from Harvard magna cum laude and a member of the Phi Beta Kappa honor society; he ranked twenty-first of 177 students in his class. At the urging of a professor and his girlfriend Alice Lee, whom he later married, Theodore gave up his ambition to become a naturalist and decided instead to attend law school, with the goal of entering public service. He entered Columbia Law School in 1880 but dropped out a year later because of his distaste for the law. He never sought admission to the bar.

After leaving law school, Roosevelt became the youngest candidate to ever be elected to the New York State Assembly at the age of twenty-three. In 1882 Theodore joined the National Guard and was commissioned as a second lieutenant; he was promoted to captain the following year. Theodore experienced a double tragedy in 1882, when his mother died of typhoid fever and hours later, in the same house, his wife died from Bright's disease, a chronic kidney infection. He wrote in his diary, "The light has gone out of my life."

Theodore got married again a few years later, and he went on to serve on the U.S. Civil Service Commission. He served as New York Police Commissioner and as President of the N.Y. Police Board before being appointed Assistant Secretary of the Navy in 1897. The next year Roosevelt served as lieutenant colonel of the "Rough Riders," and was promoted to colonel in the Spanish-American War. He became Governor of New York in 1898, and then he was elected as William McKinley's second vice president. One year into President McKinley's second term the president was shot and Theodore Roosevelt became the twenty-fifth President of the United States.

Theodore Roosevelt was the first American to be awarded the Nobel Peace Prize for mediating the Russo-Japanese War. During his administration, he worked to extend the presidential authority while making the United States a world power. Among the many highlights in this man's life, it should be noted that as president he boxed regularly with sparring partners until he lost his eyesight in his left eye. In addition, by the time he died at the age of sixty-one, he had written thirty books.

More Information About Theodore Roosevelt	
State Represented	New York
Party Affiliation	Republican
Siblings	Second of Four Children
School(s) Attended	Harvard College, Columbia Law School
Occupation(s)	Military Officer, New York Police Commissioner
Hobbies	Reading, Writing, Boxing
Pet	Macaw, Pony
Political Particulars in Office	Established Departments of Commerce and Labor; Signed treaty to build Panama Canal; Established National Forest Service and made first federal game preserve; Won Nobel Peace Prize for negotiating the Portsmouth Treaty that ended the Russo-Japanese War; Established first National Monuments
States in Union During Teenage Years	Thirty-eight

WILLIAM HOWARD TAFT

Twenty-Seventh President of the United States
Lived: 1857 – 1930   Served: 1909 – 1913

William Howard Taft was the heaviest of all the presidents, weighing in at close to three hundred and fifty pounds. At six feet, two inches tall he had grown so bulky that he got stuck in the White House bathtub and had to have an oversized model brought in for his use. He was also the only president who had a handlebar mustache.

William was born in Cincinnati, Ohio. He was the seventh of his father's ten children; the second of five children from his father's second marriage. His father, a prominent attorney, had already distinguished himself by being Secretary of War and Attorney General under President Grant. William's father demanded of his sons enthusiastic hard work, first rank in their classes, and careers in law wherever they went. William's mother was the daughter of a merchant. She was strong-willed and efficient. She once wrote, "I am more and more impressed with the responsibility of training children properly. I find that Willie needs constant watching and correcting, and it requires great caution and firmness to do the right thing always. It seems to me there can be no stronger motive for improvement than the thought of the influence on our children." All five of her sons were outstanding students at Yale University.

William was a fun-loving, active, and well-behaved child. He was an avid baseball player who was a good second baseman and power hitter but, because of his size, a poor base runner. He also took dancing lessons twice a week and, despite his bulk, was relatively light on his feet. He and his friends enjoyed swimming and ice-skating in an idle canal. He joined other kids in stone-throwing warfare against a rival gang. At the age of nine he fractured his skull and almost died when a horse ran away with the carriage in which he was riding.

Taft learned the fundamentals at the sixteenth district public school in Cincinnati. He was a good student, invariably placing at or near the top of his class. At Woodward High School he took the college preparatory curriculum; he graduated second in the class of 1874 (when he ranked fifth after one school period, his father had commented, "Mediocrity will not do for Will").

In 1874, at the age of seventeen, William entered Yale University where he became, according to a classmate, "the most admired and respected man not only in my class, but in all Yale." His school buddies tried to get William to play football for the school team, but by now he had decided not to participate in too many extracurricular activities. His father had warned him that sports would only divert him from study. He did, however, represent his freshman class in an intramural wrestling match. He also joined the Skull and Bones Society and was elected junior class orator. Taft won a math prize in his junior year and composition prizes in his senior year. He later credited Yale for shaping much of his character and singled out Professor William Graham Sumner for stimulating his intellect.

"Big Bill" won his greatest fame in college as the best debater at Yale, and he received the highest tribute from his class when he was elected class orator for their commencement exercises. His rank as second scholar in his class gave him the title of class salutatorian, and he delivered his oration in Latin at the commencement exercises of 1878.

Taft was popular with all the students and professors throughout his college career. He was popular with the "grinds" since he studied hard and fought for first place in scholarship from start to finish with the best students. At the same time he was a "jolly good fellow" and was well liked among the boys who didn't neglect to have a good time in school, but he was always self-restrained and was never mixed up in any escapades during college.

After graduating from Yale, William began studying law at the University of Cincinnati Law School. After graduating, he began practicing law while he worked as a court reporter for the Cincinnati Times, writing up the court news for the newspaper.

In 1882, at age twenty-five, President Arthur appointed Taft Collector of Internal Revenue for the first district of Ohio. He then became a superior court judge. President Benjamin Harrison appointed Taft to the position of Solicitor General of the United States, and then appointed him a federal circuit judge. While still a judge, he became a Dean of Law at the University of Cincinnati. In 1901 President McKinley appointed William chief civil administrator of the Philippine Islands. He was then selected as Secretary of War by President Theodore Roosevelt. In 1909, at the age of fifty-two, William Howard Taft became the twenty-seventh President of the United States.

Taft's story doesn't end there. He much preferred law to politics, and although he did not get re-elected after one term in office, William went on to work as a professor of law at Yale University. In 1921, at the age of sixty-four, Taft attained the position he had aspired to all his life — President Harding appointed him Chief Justice of the United States Supreme Court.

More Information About William H. Taft

State Represented	Ohio
Party Affiliation	Republican
Siblings	Seventh of Ten Children
School(s) Attended	Yale College, Cincinnati Law School
Occupation(s)	Federal Circuit Judge; Professor of Law at Yale
Hobbies	Baseball, Swimming, Ice-Skating, Dancing, Wrestling
Pet	Cow
Political Particulars In Office	Payne-Aldrich Tariff Act, Dollar Diplomacy, Vigorous enforcement of the Anti-trust policy, First President of 48 contiguous States, 16th Amendment (Income Tax)
States in Union During Teenage Years	Thirty-eight

WOODROW WILSON

Twenty-Eighth President of the United States
Lived: 1856 – 1924   Served: 1913 – 1921

Woodrow Wilson was the most highly educated man ever to become president, having received more than a dozen degrees and written many scholarly books. He is the only president who has ever received a Ph.D.

Woodrow was born in Staunton, Virginia just four years before the American Civil War began. He had two older sisters and younger brother, and his father was a Presbyterian minister and a brilliant theology professor. He once told his son, "The roast beef of hard industry gives blood for climbing the ladder of life." An atmosphere of religious piety and scholarly interests dominated Wilson's early years. Woodrow's mother was a very caring and loving person who was educated in the seminary. Wilson was once quoted as saying, "I remember how I clung to her (laughed at as a 'momma's boy') 'til I was a great big fellow, but love of the best womanhood came to me and entered my heart through those apron strings." He clung to those apron strings until he married Ellen Louise Axson at the age of twenty-eight.

Wilson was a thin, high-strung child who had to wear glasses and was, according to his mother, "a mischievous bundle of nerves." Before he was two, his family moved to Georgia where his father accepted a job as a minister. Between the ages of four and eight, Wilson lived in an atmosphere colored by the Civil War, which strained families throughout the nation. Food became scarce and Woodrow found himself having to drink cowpea soup every day. Cowpeas had always been thought of only as food for cows, but as his father said, "wartime means sacrifice." During the war, Woodrow's father sided with the South. He constantly worried about two of his brothers who were Union generals. Although Woodrow left the region as a young adult he, throughout his life, regarded himself as a southerner. He, like his father, believed that the South was fully justified in seceding from the Union, and he believed in white supremacy.

Woodrow was thought to be a slow learner as a young child. He was unable to read until age nine and he had trouble grasping fundamental arithmetic. His weak eyes and frail health undermined his efforts at improvement. However, he was not uneducated. His father taught the boy at home, and they read countless stories from the bible and many books by Charles Dickens. Woodrow's father constantly told him to "Learn to think on your feet. Choose your words wisely, and then shoot straight at the target. Don't mumble and fumble."

Formal schooling was a major readjustment for young Woodrow. He didn't start until he was nine. He did not take quickly to sitting on wooden chairs and writing on desktops; he much preferred the comfort of a soft sofa or parlor floor at home. In addition, instruction from the strict headmaster, with his endless lists of Latin verbs, countless lessons in penmanship, and lengthy history orations, lacked the eloquence of his father's lectures.

On weekdays Woodrow's father took him to visit a corn mill, a cotton gin, or some other plant. After these trips they had to discuss what they had seen, because Wilson's father believed the exact expression of ideas was necessary for clear understanding.

When the school was moved to a spot near the river, more avenues of exploring and adventure opened up. With opportunities to spend his time swimming, playing baseball, or just walking in the woods, Woodrow's formal education all but disappeared completely. Even the wax cane that the headmaster used frequently, and with careful aim, did little to stimulate interest in formal education in Woodrow and his classmates.

In 1870, when Woodrow was fourteen, his father became a professor in a seminary in South Carolina. The increase in salary afforded more attractive educational opportunities for his four children. With a key to the seminary library that his father gave him, Woodrow embarked on a personal journey of learning designed to find subjects that interested him that he could be enthusiastic about. He could not get enough of American and British history; he also enjoyed biographies of notable figures and taught himself effective shorthand.

Despite his zest for learning, Woodrow failed to win any major scholastic honors, but he did acquire a strong self-discipline that proved valuable throughout his life. Always partial to his father's teaching, Woodrow frequently visited the seminary classrooms to take in lectures and discussions. Because much of the formal learning he had in the past relied upon memorization, a talent Woodrow lacked, he welcomed hearing presentations that could be talked about, analyzed and applied.

There was little doubt about who Woodrow's hero was during his formative years; his father was his friend, mentor, and advisor. He was a fountain of knowledge and wisdom, and he offered spiritual inspiration and direction for the family. Woodrow's mother provided love and sensitivity, as well as a gentle and quiet awareness of the importance of people in the world around her and their human needs.

When Woodrow was sixteen, he entered Davidson College in Charlotte, North Carolina, to prepare himself for the ministry. The college still suffered from the effects of the Civil War. The grueling entrance tests revealed that Woodrow was lacking in several subjects, including geography, Latin, Greek, and mathematics, so he was placed on probation.

Woodrow won the greatest attention and respect of both teachers and peers when he took part in debates. Having grown up in a home with both formal and informal training in speaking, paid rich dividends, and he won membership in the school debating club. He displayed polished technical skills, and an ability to think quickly on his feet. "You seem born to orate," one professor noted, a comment hardly wasted on a young man seeking confidence in a school where he often felt less bright than those around him.

Even though he had to study a little harder, Woodrow could not pass up the opportunity to take part in extracurricular activities. He joined the glee club and earned a spot on the baseball team playing center field. He left Davidson after his freshman year due to illness, and spent the next fourteen months regaining his health.

At the age of nineteen he enrolled at Princeton University in New Jersey. He was an intense and hardworking student. Science and math continued to pull his grades down, but he still managed to graduate thirty-eighth of 167 students. Wilson practiced public speaking, became a leader in debating, and continued to read about the lives of great British statesmen. In extracurricular activities he contributed historical articles to the literary magazine and was editor of *The Princetonian*. He joined the American Whig Society Debating Club, and organized the Liberal Debating Club for students to discuss political questions of the present century. He was president of the baseball association and secretary of the football association. He played Marc Anthony in the satirical sketch "The Sanguinary Tragedy of Julius Sneezer." His ambition was for a career in politics – in college he had cards printed that read, "Thomas Woodrow Wilson, Senator from Virginia."

In 1879 Wilson entered the University of Virginia Law School, but he dropped out in his second year, again for health reasons. He got bored with legal study, having pursued it only as a means to enter politics. He preferred extracurricular activities at the Charlottesville campus. He was president of the Jefferson Literary Society Debating Club, and he won the orator's prize when he argued the negative side of the debate: "is the Roman Catholic Church a menace to American institutions?" He also sang tenor in the glee club and a college quartet at the law school. While recuperating at home in Wilmington, North Carolina, Wilson continued to study law on his own and was admitted to the bar in October, 1882.

Wilson pursued even more education, and received a Ph.D degree in political science from Johns Hopkins University at the age of thirty. In addition, he earned Doctor of Law and Doctor of Literature degrees from Yale University. He also organized the Johns Hopkins Glee Club. After practicing law for less than a year he decided to give it up, along with his dream of a career in politics, to become an educator.

After being a very successful and popular professor for a number of years, Wilson became president of Princeton University. He then went on to become Governor of New Jersey, and then served two-terms as President of the United States.

As president, Woodrow Wilson pushed a lot of legislation through Congress, but his administration was dominated by the declaration of war against Germany in 1917, which officially involved the United States in World War I. Wilson pushed for the signing of the Treaty of Versailles in 1919, which effectively ended the war and brought to fruition his dream of establishing a League of Nations, which has since been replaced with the United Nations.

More Information About Woodrow Wilson	
Born & Lived	Born in Virginia; Lived in Georgia, South Carolina, North Carolina, Connecticut, Maryland
State Represented	New Jersey
Party Affiliation	Democrat
Siblings	Third of Four Children
School(s) Attended	Davidson College, Princeton University, University of Virginia Law School, Johns Hopkins University, Yale University
Occupation(s)	College professor, president of Princeton University
Hobbies	Swimming, Playing Baseball, Walking, Singing, Debating/Public Speaking
Pet	Sheep
Political Particulars in Office	Established Federal Trade Commission; World War I; Treaty of Versailles; Established League of Nations
States in Union During Teenage Years	Thirty-seven

WARREN G. HARDING

Twenty-Ninth President of the United States
Lived: 1865 – 1923   Served: 1921 – 1923

Warren Harding has the unfortunate distinction of being rated the worst president the United States has ever had by a group of distinguished historians. As the dark horse Republican candidate, he won the presidential election by the largest majority in history: sixty-one percent of the popular vote. It was the first election in which women were allowed to vote. It is said that he was the most handsome president, and there doesn't seem to be any doubt that much of his success in politics was based on his good looks.

Warren was born on a farm in Corsica, Ohio, the year the American Civil War ended in 1865. He was the oldest of four sisters and one brother. His father was a farmer and horse trader with a talent for veterinary work. When Warren was eight-years-old, his father completed a quick course in homeopathic medicine. He supplemented his small income by becoming a homeopathic doctor, and he often took his son on horse and buggy calls.

Warren's mother was a deeply religious woman who became a devout Seventh Day Adventist. On the basis of her experience as a midwife, and from assisting her husband in his medical practice, she was granted a license to practice medicine. Unlike so many other presidential mothers, Warren's mother had no particular strength of character. One day his father said to him, "Warren, it's a good thing you weren't born a gal." "Why?" Warren asked. "Because you would be in the family way all the time. You can't say NO!"

Although Harding spoke fondly of his rural upbringing, the truth was that he did not like farm chores. As a small boy, he milked cows, groomed horses, and painted barns. He formed a secret club with his pals to compete with the Chain Gang. As a hired hand, he helped grade the roadbed of the Toledo and Ohio Central Railroad. He also learned to play the cornet in the village band.

More importantly for his later career, Warren worked as a printer's devil (an apprentice in a printer's office) at the weekly newspaper when he was twelve-years-old. It fascinated him, and he was determined to know all there was to know about running a newspaper. He gradually learned how to set type, how to run a printing press, and in time he became the owner of a newspaper.

Warren's health was generally poor. At age twenty-four he suffered a nervous breakdown and spent several weeks in a sanitarium in Battle Creek, Michigan. He returned to the sanitarium many times during his life because of "frazzled" nerves.

Warren's mother taught him to memorize and recite poetry even before sending him off to Blooming Grove's one-room schoolhouse with its McGuffey's Readers (first illustrated reading books for children in the first six grades). From an early age he enjoyed standing up in front of the class to perform excerpts from famous speeches or poems.

Warren attended grammar schools in Corsica and Caledonia in Ohio. Although he was not much of a scholar, his mother sent him to Ohio Central College at the age of fourteen to study the ministry and become a preacher. One of sixty students there, he studied such traditional subjects as Latin, math, history, and chemistry, but he excelled in debating and composition. He disliked the study of chemistry and once put a bottle of awful smelling hydrogen sulfide in his teacher's desk drawer. Drawing on his printing background Warren helped launch a campus newspaper that he edited, he served as editor of the yearbook, and he played the cornet and alto horn in a brass band. At the age of seventeen, he graduated with a Bachelor's degree in Science, and delivered the commencement address.

Harding was not interested in the ministry, and was not sure what he wanted to do with his life. He read little besides a daily news digest and personal letters. During school vacations, he took what employment he could find: he worked in a sawmill, as a broom-maker, and as a railroad construction laborer.

Presidents Were Teenagers Too

Soon after graduation, at age seventeen, he began teaching in a country school, for which he got $30 a month. He only did this for one term because he found it too difficult to educate big farm boys. Later he called teaching, "the hardest job I ever had."

In the early days Warren expected to become a lawyer, even though his mother wanted him to be a preacher. He studied law for a while and tried hard to get interested, but he found that it was too dull for him. He then tried selling insurance but did not like that either. He preferred shooting pool and playing poker with the town sportsmen. His greatest early success came when he helped organize the Citizen's Cornet Band of Marion, Ohio.

Finally, Warren turned back to journalism. He entered a newspaper office and became a reporter. Here was action and adventure, and after a little while he decided that this would be his life's work. He first worked at the *Marion Democratic Mirror*, at age nineteen, and earned $1 a week. But he was fired after being there just a few weeks for being an enthusiastic supporter of James E. Blain, the Republican candidate for president.

With his newfound love of newspaper work, Harding persuaded two unemployed friends to join him in scraping together $300 to take over a bankrupt daily newspaper, *The Marion Star*. Eventually his two partners dropped out of the business and Warren became the sole owner. His paper supported Republican politicians, which enabled him to get support from wealthy Republican donors. Battling with two other local newspapers for advertising dollars, the tobacco-chewing Harding joined in the rough and tumble journalism of the times that disregarded laws of libel and took part in mudslinging at rivals.

By the end of the 1890's, Warren's newspaper had become a financial success and an influential voice in Republican affairs. As editor and publisher, he made regular appearances as a speaker in political campaigns. His oratory skills and handsome appearance made politicians think of him as a likely candidate for office.

With prodding and encouragement from the political machine and his wife Florence Kling, Warren was elected to the Ohio Legislature. He went on to win an election as lieutenant governor, but he ran unsuccessfully for governor. Six years later he served two terms as a United States Senator. As a dark horse candidate in 1920, he won the Republican nomination for president on the tenth ballot.

Harding won the presidential election in a landslide, but his administration did not go quite as smoothly. His term in office was essentially run by the Republican political machine, and two years after starting in office, while on a trip campaigning for the Republican Party in San Francisco, California, he became ill and died of a heart attack. He died just before many members of his cabinet were convicted and were sent to prison. His administration was probably the most scandal-ridden of any president. There are, in fact, some conspiracy theorists who believe Harding was poisoned. Warren's wife refused to allow an autopsy and burned all of his public and private papers.

More Information About Warren G. Harding	
State Represented	Ohio
Party Affiliation	Republican
Siblings	First of six Children
School(s) Attended	Ohio Central College
Occupation(s)	Insurance Salesman, Reporter, Newspaper Publisher & Owner
Hobbies	Shooting Pool, Playing Poker, Playing in a Brass Band
Pet	Dog: Airedale Terrier named Laddie Boy
Political Particulars In Office	Died in office
States in Union During Teenage Years	Thirty-eight

CALVIN COOLIDGE

Thirtieth President of the United States
Lived: 1872 – 1933   Served: 1923 – 1929

Calvin Coolidge was the seventh vice president to become president upon the death of a president. He was the only president who was sworn in by his father who was a notary public, among the many other titles he held as a public official. As president, Calvin Coolidge slept eleven hours a day. He went to bed at ten, got up between seven and nine, and always took an afternoon nap lasting two to four hours. He was a man of sharp wit and very few words.

Calvin was born on Independence Day, July 4, 1872, in Plymouth, Vermont. He had only one other sibling, a younger sister, who died when she was nine. Calvin's father was a farmer, a village storeowner, and a local public official. He also served six years in the Vermont House of Representatives and one term in the State Senate. Very little is known about Calvin's mother except that she was a very loving and caring person. She was also a very frail woman who became an invalid in her thirties and died when Calvin was twelve. "The greatest grief that can come to a boy, came to me," he said later. "She used what strength she had to lavish care upon me and my sister." For the rest of his life Coolidge carried his mother's picture on the back of his watch.

As a young boy, Calvin assisted in his father's store as well as on the family farm. A sober, dependable child, he helped out with many chores, such as plowing and stacking wood. In his autobiography he said, "After milking cows in the morning, the fences had to be repaired where they had been broken by the snow, the cattle turned out to pasture, and the spring planting done. Then came sheep-shearing time, which was followed by getting in the hay, harvesting and threshing of the grain, cutting and husking the corn, digging the potatoes, and picking the apples." His favorite work on the farm, though, was tapping and processing maple sugar.

Coolidge explained more about his work on the farm, "I early learned to drive oxen and used to plow with them alone when I was twelve-years-old. There was also the constant care of the domestic animals, and taking the cows to and from pasture, which was especially my responsibility." He earned spare cash selling apples and popcorn balls at town meetings, and while a student, making toys at a local carriage shop. His early ambition was to be a storekeeper like his father.

His father knew that when he told Calvin to do something, it would always get done; his work was never left incomplete and he never had to be told twice. All his various chores occupied the beginning and end of each day. After he went away to school, Calvin returned at planting time to help his father. He put on the working frock and boots that had been worn by his grandfather, and "then there would be some plowing done." In the store young Calvin learned a lot about various kinds of human behavior. He heard men exchange public judgments as well as share their shrewd and humorous analyses of personal character and passing events.

Calvin also learned a lot at home, "We had some books, but not many. Mother liked poetry and read some novels. Father had no taste for books, but always read a daily paper. My grandmother Coolidge liked books… and read aloud to me…. She also had two volumes entitled *Washington and His Generals*, and other biographies which I read myself at an early age with a great deal of interest."

The loss of his mother was devastating to Calvin, and things got harder still when his sister passed away at age fifteen from appendicitis. He was without strong feminine influence during most of his adolescent years. It was to his advantage that both of the secondary schools he attended were co-educational, but he was not one who easily made the acquaintance of girls.

In a remarkable period of self-revelation, Calvin once explained to a friend how difficult it had been for him as a boy to meet people. "Most of the visitors would sit with father and mother in the kitchen, and the hardest thing in the world was to have to go through the kitchen door and give them a greeting. By fighting hard, I used to manage to get through that door. I'm all right with old friends, but every time I meet a stranger, I have to go through the old kitchen door, and it's not easy."

From ages five to twelve Coolidge attended the local elementary school a mile from his home in Plymouth. He was a fair student and behaved satisfactorily. He studied under teachers whose strength and personal worth he praised, and he always had his father's careful supervision. At school Calvin showed no remarkable aptitude, but at the age of thirteen he passed the examination qualifying him to teach. From the time he was thirteen until he was seventeen, Calvin attended Black River Academy in Ludlow, Vermont, twelve miles from his home. His lonely father drove the distance in a horse-drawn wagon almost every weekend to be with his son.

"During my first term at Black River Academy, I began algebra and finished grammar. For some reason, I was attracted to civil government and took that. This was my first introduction to the Constitution of the United States. Although I was only fourteen-years-old, the subject interested me exceedingly." Calvin also explained, "Going away to school was the first great adventure of my life. I shall never forget the impression it made on me. It was the same when I went to college. What I studied was the result of my own choice. Instead of seeking to direct me, my father left me to decide. But when I had selected a course he was always attentive to see that I diligently applied myself to it."

While at Black River Academy, Calvin continued to receive average marks and was class secretary at the time of his graduation in the nine-member class of 1890. He delivered the commencement address entitled *The Oratory in History.*

After failing the entrance examination for Amherst College, Calvin took college preparatory instruction at the St. Johnsbury Academy before finally being admitted to Amherst in 1891, at the age of nineteen. He was an average student during his first two years at college, because he found that learning to debate and make speeches was more important to him than his studies. But from his junior year on Calvin improved markedly, taking a special interest in rhetoric, history, and philosophy. He also studied modern and ancient languages, becoming quite proficient in Greek, in math from algebra to calculus, and in literature. His worst grade was a D in physics. His favorite instructor was a philosophy professor who greatly influenced Coolidge's social values and encouraged his interest in public service.

Calvin was a loner on campus – he did not participate in sports and he took part in few extracurricular activities. He also waited until his senior year to join a fraternity.

In 1892, at the age of twenty, Calvin joined the Republican Party and supported the re-nomination of President Benjamin Harrison. For his senior essay, *The Principles Fought for in the American Revolution*, Coolidge won first prize and a $150 gold medal in a national contest. Having earned a reputation as the campus wit, Calvin was chosen by his fellow students to deliver the Grove Oration, traditionally a sarcastic, satirical commencement address. Coolidge graduated cum laude from Amherst College in 1895 at the age of twenty-three.

After graduation Calvin studied law, and he was admitted to the bar in 1897 at age twenty-five. After practicing law for a short while, he became very active in local politics. He methodically climbed the political ladder, starting as a councilman in North Hampton, Massachusetts, and going on to become mayor, a state senator, lieutenant governor, and governor of Massachusetts. He became Vice President of the United States, and finally, upon the untimely death of President Warren Harding during his second term, Calvin Coolidge became the thirtieth President of the United States. As president, he was a man of so few words that he was given the nickname "Silent Cal."

In a tragic accident during his presidential campaign, Coolidge's youngest son, at age sixteen, developed an infection on the heel of his foot after playing a game of tennis in sneakers without socks. A few days later he died of blood poisoning. In his autobiography Calvin wrote, "When he went, the power and glory of the presidency went with him." Coolidge decided not to run for re-election, simply saying, "I do not choose to run for president in 1928."

More Information About Calvin Coolidge

Born	Vermont
State Represented	Massachusetts
Party Affiliation	Republican
Siblings	First of Two Children
School(s) Attended	Amherst College
Occupation(s)	Lawyer
Hobbies	Fishing, Golfing, Pitching Hay, Debate, Oratory, Pranks
Pet	Dog named Rob Roy
Political Particulars in Office	Nicknamed "Silent Cal"
States in Union During Teen-age Years	Forty-four

HERBERT CLARK HOOVER

Thirty-First President of the United States
Lived: 1874 – 1964 Served: 1929 – 1933

Herbert Hoover never held an elected office until he was elected President of the United States. He was the only president whose profession was engineering. Herbert Hoover was president during the worst economic depression this country has had to date.

Herbert was the first president born west of the Mississippi River. He and his older brother and younger sister were born in West Branch, Iowa. Their father was a successful blacksmith and a farm equipment salesman, who also served as town assessor and councilman. He died at the age of thirty-three from typhoid fever, when Herbert was only six. He left a $1,000 life insurance policy and a little property to his wife.

At age two Herbert nearly died of the croup. He had a hoarse, ringing cough and had difficulty breathing; his vital signs were unnoticeable to his parents, and they gave him up for dead, placing pennies over his eyes and drawing a sheet over his face. Fortunately Herbert's uncle, Dr. John Minthorn, arrived in time to revive him. Herbert subsequently contracted more typical childhood diseases like measles, mumps and chicken pox. He once stepped barefoot on a hot iron chip in his father's blacksmith shop; the incident permanently scarred the sole of his foot. At age six Herbert recalled hurling a flaming stick into a hot cauldron of tar, sending billows of thick black smoke all over town.

When his father died in 1880, Herbert was periodically sent to stay with relatives in order to ease the burden on his mother. He lived briefly with one uncle in his pioneer sod house in Iowa. At age seven Hoover spent an exciting seven months living with another uncle who was superintendent of the Osage Indian reservation in Pawhuska, Oklahoma Territory. There Herbert played with Indian children and learned how to hunt with a bow and arrow, among other native survival skills.

Herbert's mother was a fortunate woman in her time – she was able to attend college and she taught school for a while. She was a strong advocate for women's rights. She became a Quaker minister and preached at meetings all over Iowa. Returning home from a Quaker meeting one night she caught cold and, at age thirty-six, died of pneumonia. Herbert was nine-years-old when his mother died, leaving him and his siblings orphans.

With the death of their mother in 1883, the three Hoover children were divided among relatives. Herbert went with his Uncle Allan Hoover who had a farm outside town, but the next year he was passed to Dr. John Minthorn, the uncle who had saved his life as an infant, and whose own son had recently died.

In 1888, when Herbert was fourteen, they moved to Salem, Oregon. Hoover helped with many of the chores, such as clearing the fields, chopping wood and tending the horses. Although an orphan, Herbert had a pleasant childhood. He played in the woods, and fished and swam in the streams. He picked potato bugs to earn money to buy fireworks – he received a penny for every hundred bugs he picked. He also earned spare cash picking strawberries and collecting scrap iron. As a child, Hoover dreamed of becoming a railroad engineer, but he also had an interest in geology, as he often examined the stone collection of his dentist, Dr. William Walker.

During his early years Hoover received his education at the West Branch free school in the town where he was born. An average student, he later recalled that the only part of school he liked was recess. Having been raised with a strong religious influence, Herbert had read the entire bible by age ten. Other than an encyclopedia, there were few books in his home.

After moving to Oregon, Herbert attended the Friends Pacific Academy for two years in Newberg, where he continued to receive average grades in most subjects, but he excelled in math. He received his secondary school education at Newberg College, a small Quaker academy where his uncle was principal. Herbert attended the school from the time he was eleven until he was fifteen, but he never actually graduated from high school.

Hoover quit school at the age of fifteen and went to work in his uncle's new real estate office where, by accident, he met a schoolteacher who was an advisor to schoolchildren in her spare time. Herbert's love of reading was sparked by this stranger, Miss Jeannie Gray of Salem, Oregon. She introduced him to a variety of books, and he remained indebted to her for the rest of his life for her continued interest in his reading material. He expressed his lifetime gratitude in the July, 1959 issue of Reader's Digest, when Hoover was eighty-five-years-old. The title read, "Thank You, Miss Gray!"

Herbert studied algebra and geometry at a local business college at night. In 1890, at age sixteen, he became interested in engineering after talking with an engineer who visited his uncle's office.

Having failed the entrance examination in all areas except math for the newly established Stanford University in California, Herbert was forced to take college preparatory instruction. Tested again, he passed but was admitted "conditionally" in English, a condition removed during his senior year. At age seventeen he was the youngest student in Stanford's first class in 1891. Under the university's pass-fail system of evaluation, Hoover, a geology major, received passing grades in all subjects except German. In extracurricular activities, he was elected junior class treasurer and treasurer of the student body, he played shortstop on the freshman baseball team, and was manager of the baseball and football teams. During Herbert's junior year, former President Benjamin Harrison came to Stanford to deliver a series of lectures, and Hoover was fortunate to make his acquaintance.

Herbert worked to earn money whenever he could. One summer he weeded onions for fifty cents a day. Hoover worked his way through Stanford as a newsboy and clerk in the registration office, and he started a student laundry service. During the summer between his freshman and sophomore years he worked as an assistant on the Geological Survey of Arkansas, mapping out the north side of the Ozark Mountains.

The next two summers he worked with the U.S. Geological Survey in California and Nevada. Hoover graduated with an A.B. in geology at the age of twenty-one, in 1895, and he decided to become a mining engineer.

Unable to find work as an engineer after graduation, Herbert took a $2.00-a-day job as a gold miner's helper in the goldfields of Nevada.

Before long he decided to join his brother, who was working as a linotype operator, in order to support their younger sister. While there he visited the office of Louis Janin, a leading mining engineer, and when told there were no engineering jobs available, Herbert accepted work as a typing assistant for $150 a month.

In 1896, at age twenty-two, Herbert went to San Francisco where he was hired by a firm of mining engineers. He started as an office boy, but in less than a year he was an assistant to the superintendent of one of the company's mines.

When he was twenty-four-years-old, Herbert married Lou Henry, his college sweetheart and the only female geology student at Stanford, who was the daughter of a wealthy banker. They had two children. They traveled the world together, working, learning new languages, and providing aid to those in need.

After working for various mining companies, including working as the lead engineer for a private corporation in China, Hoover formed his own engineering firm at the age of thirty-four, which aided in unearthing resources all over the world. By this point he identified with the progressive wing of the Republican Party and contributed $1,000 to Theodore Roosevelt's third-party bid for president in 1912.

Hoover gained international attention when he became very involved in the relief efforts during World War I. He became an important war-time advisor to President Woodrow Wilson, even though he was a Republican, and was appointed head of the U.S. Food Administration, the organization that allocated America's food resources during the conflict. Herbert organized and administered several private relief efforts before, during, and after the war, including capably serving as a member of the Supreme Economic Council and as head of the American Relief Administration.

In 1921 Hoover was selected to be Secretary of Commerce by President Warren Harding, and was retained in that position by President Calvin Coolidge. He served with distinction and, with his steady rise in Republican politics and in the public domain, was chosen to be the Republican nominee for the presidency in 1928. His Democratic opponent was Alfred Smith, a four-term Governor from New York and the first Catholic to run for president. Hoover won the election easily, with fifty-eight percent of the vote. Although President Hoover did many good things during his administration, his term in office was dominated by the stock market crash and the Great Depression of 1929, which ultimately brought him down.

More Information About Herbert Hoover

Born & Lived	b. Iowa; l. Oregon
State Represented	California
Party Affiliation	Republican
Siblings	Second of Three Children
School(s) Attended	Stanford University
Occupation(s)	Mining Engineer, Administrator
Hobbies	Fishing, Swimming, Reading, Baseball
Pet	Dog named King Tut
Political Particulars in Office	Great Depression of 1929
States in Union During Teenage Years	Forty-four

FRANKLIN DELANO ROOSEVELT

Thirty-Second President of the United States
Lived: 1882 – 1945   Served: 1933 – 1945

Franklin Delano Roosevelt was the only president who had a crippling disease, poliomyelitis, which paralyzed him from the waist down. He is also the only president to have been re-elected to third and fourth terms – a greater honor and trust than ever given any other man (the twenty-second amendment, which set the two-term limit for the presidency, was passed after FDR was elected to his fourth term in 1944). Franklin's fifth cousin, Theodore Roosevelt, was the twenty-sixth President of the United States.

FDR was born on his father's estate in a thirty-five-room mansion in Hyde Park, New York. When Franklin was born, there was a short time when it was thought that both mother and child might die. After many long hours of labor the baby had not come, so the doctor administered chloroform, an overdose as it turned out, to Franklin's mother. She fell unconscious and turned blue for a time, and when the baby came he was also unconscious and blue. Only with mouth-to-mouth resuscitation by the doctor did this future President of the United States survive. Franklin weighed ten pounds at birth.

Franklin's father was an attorney and a wealthy executive of one railroad company, and a director of two other railroad companies. Franklin's mother was a member of the wealthy Delano family. When FDR was born, his mother was twenty-six-years-old and his father was fifty-four. Franklin was his father's second son and the only child

112

from his second marriage; his half brother was twenty-eight, two years older than his mother, when Franklin was born.

FDR's parents brought him up with loving firmness. His mother made him live by a rigid schedule – she set definite times for daily activities such as eating, studying and playing. She was very domineering, and even after her son was grown and had children of his own, she reminded him to put on his boots before going outdoors in rainy weather. Franklin's father made sure his son had all the advantages that wealth could buy, but he also taught Franklin that being wealthy brought with it the responsibility of helping people who were not so lucky.

As a child, Franklin wore dresses until he was five, and then he wore skirts until age seven when he began wearing pants. At age four, his father gave him a pony, and he learned to ride as soon as he could sit on it. At eight-years-old, Franklin was permitted to take his first unsupervised bath. When he was eleven, his father taught him to hunt with a rifle. Franklin also learned to skate, to play tennis, and to sail – he liked to go out on his father's yacht. The captain taught him how to sail, and at age sixteen he got his own sailboat.

When Franklin was six, his father took him to the White House to meet President Grover Cleveland. It was reported that President Cleveland patted Franklin on the head and said, "My little man, I am making a strange wish for you. It is that you may *never* be President of the United States."

Roosevelt's youth, however, was not wholly frivolous. He read a great deal (Mark Twain was his favorite author), and he early acquired his mother's and his "uncle" Theodore's love for the sea. He was exposed in his private education to wider, more liberal dimensions of social thought and conscience, principally through his Swiss governess.

Franklin's parents also joined in his education. Franklin's mother read stories to him when he was young. Once he learned to read he sat for hours and poured over books about sea battles. At age twelve he had read all the books on sea power by Captain Alfred Mahan, whose books were also being read by the admirals of the world's naval powers. His early ambition was to attend Annapolis and become a career naval officer, but his father encouraged him to take up law.

Franklin did not go to schools, public or private, in his early years. Like many children of rich parents, nurses, governesses and tutors taught him at home. At an early age he could converse in French and

German. He liked taking dance lessons but detested his piano and drawing lessons. He had special times set aside for study and play, but there were no specific times for chores or work.

Franklin's favorite place in Hyde Park was the family library, where books stood floor to ceiling. He read the books shelf by shelf. When magazines came from overseas, Franklin ran off with them. "And what he reads," his proud mother told friends, "he seems to remember with a memory that's like flypaper – everything sticks to it." Franklin seemed eager to cast out a wide net and gather as many things as possible to study and master. He walked in the woods and studied the trees, and with his father he studied all the birds in the countryside.

At age fifteen Franklin's father gave him a camera. Franklin took the camera apart and studied how each part worked. When he took pictures, he developed the film himself in a basement darkroom. Some of Franklin's hobbies included photography, stamp collecting, studying birds, and forestry. He kept up with these interests throughout his life.

From the time he was three-years-old, Franklin went with his parents on their annual trips to Europe. Roosevelt attended a public school only once, for six weeks during a family trip to Germany. His mother thought the experience might improve his German. When Franklin was fourteen-years-old, he and his tutor bought bicycles and took off together on a tour of Germany – his parents told them to meet them in Belgium!

Most of the time Franklin was a happy boy, but sometimes he did get lonely. Neighborhood children came to play with him, but he didn't have many friends. He had spent so much time with his father and mother that he did not know how to play with other children.

At age fourteen Roosevelt entered Groton School, a private college preparatory school in Groton, Massachusetts. Franklin's mother was not in a hurry to send her son away to school, so he entered Groton two years later than was usual. Groton was a school for society's "wealthiest 400," where boys were trained to become leaders in business. Franklin got good grades, but was very shy. The other students laughed at the new boy because he "talked funny" – FDR had picked up a British accent during his frequent visits to Europe.

As a member of the Groton Missionary Society, Franklin directed a summer camp for disadvantaged youth. Although Franklin won prizes for punctuality and for prowess in Latin, acted in a school show, and served as manager of the baseball team, Roosevelt failed to achieve the social acceptance through success in competitive sports that he deeply craved. Franklin was not very good at sports, and he was not popular with the other boys. He graduated from Groton in 1900 at the age of eighteen. President Theodore Roosevelt, his cousin, spoke at Franklin's graduation in June of that year.

The headmaster's lessons at Groton were very different from what FDR's mother had tried to teach her son. She had different ideas about Franklin's future – she wanted him to grow up to be just like his father. After college, she wanted Franklin to go back to Hyde Park and become a country gentleman living quietly among his friends; she thought that work in government was not proper.

When Franklin heard President Theodore Roosevelt was going to invade Cuba during the Spanish-American War, he and a friend decided to run away and join the navy and Teddy Roosevelt's "Rough Riders." The scrawny Franklin did not look eighteen, but he talked a deliveryman into hiding him and his friend on a wagon when it left school the next day. That night both boys felt feverish, and the next morning both were stuck in hospital beds, ill with scarlet fever. While Franklin was quarantined, his mother got a ladder so she could stand outside his window to inspect him daily. His mother worried about him constantly. Germs seemed to strike him down more often than they hit other boys. All his life Franklin had been laid up with colds, fevers, sore throats, and earaches, but he always managed to bounce back. After several weeks in bed he recovered from the scarlet fever.

Roosevelt enrolled that same year, 1900, at Harvard University. He majored in history and government and earned C grades. Classes generally bored him, but he attended regularly. Once in a while, however, he joined other students in cutting the lecture of one biased professor by slipping out a window at the rear of the classroom. In extracurricular activities he was captain of the third crew of the New Boating Club, secretary of the glee club, librarian of Alpha Delta Phi (Fly Club), and a member of the Harvard Union Library committee. Franklin's biggest disappointment was his failure to make the football team because he was too light. He did the next best thing and became a cheerleader. His favorite activity was serving as editor-in-chief of the *Harvard Crimson,* the school newspaper. All his college activities helped him make friends more easily. He joined the Harvard Republican Club and took part in a torchlight parade in Boston for the McKinley-Roosevelt presidential ticket.

His somewhat casual scholarship notwithstanding, Franklin earned his B.A. degree in three years. But he continued his studies for another year just to work on the *Crimson,* work he later described as very useful in preparing him for public service. In his last year at Harvard he took graduate courses in history and economics, but did not earn a master's degree.

In 1904, at age twenty-two, Franklin entered Columbia University Law School, where he continued to be just an average student. He actually failed two courses, contract law and a class in pleading and practice. He had little interest in the study of law and dropped out after passing the bar examination. Roosevelt worked as a clerk in a law firm for the next three years, but he really had no enthusiasm for legal work.

Franklin married Eleanor Roosevelt, a distant cousin, at the age of twenty-three. Eleanor was the daughter of Theodore Roosevelt's brother Elliot, who had a terrible drinking problem. They had four boys and one daughter together, and she became one of the most prominent First Ladies the United States has had to date.

Prior to being president, Franklin Roosevelt served as a New York State Senator and as Assistant Secretary of the Navy under President Woodrow Wilson. It was at this time, at age thirty-nine, that Franklin was struck with polio, which put him in a wheelchair for the rest of his life. After a remarkable recovery, FDR went on to become a two-term Governor of New York, and then became the thirty-second President of the United States. He is known for asserting in his Inaugural Address, "the only thing we have to fear is fear itself." When he was re-elected for a second term, he received the largest electoral vote in the history of the presidency, 523 to 8. Franklin Delano Roosevelt died of a cerebral hemorrhage during the second year of his fourth term in office, just before the end of World War II.

More Information About Franklin D. Roosevelt	
State Represented	New York
Party Affiliation	Democrat
Siblings	Second of Two Children
School(s) Attended	Harvard University, Columbia University Law School
Occupation(s)	Lawyer
Pet	Scottish Terrier named Fala
Hobbies	Hunting, Skating, Tennis, Sailing, Swimming, Reading, Dancing, Photography, Stamp Collecting, Forestry
Political Particulars in Office	Elected to four terms in office; Led during Depression, World War II, and the attack on Pearl Harbor; Instituted New Deal program, including Social Security reform and a work relief program
States in Union During Teenage Years	Forty-five

HARRY S TRUMAN

Thirty-Third President of the United States
Lived: 1884 – 1972   Served: 1945 – 1953

Harry Truman was the seventh vice president to become President of the United States upon the death of a president. Truman was the ninth and last president to date who did not attend college. Truman is probably best known as the president who made the decision to drop atomic bombs on Hiroshima and Nagasaki to end the war with Japan in 1945.

Harry, the oldest of three children, was born in Lamar, Missouri. His father was an unsuccessful mule-trader and farmer who had very little formal schooling, yet he was self-educated. He was still working as a farmer when he died – Harry was thirty-years-old. Truman's mother grew up in a pro-Confederate household, and she never overcame her resentment of the indignities her family suffered at the hands of the North. She studied art and music at a college in Lexington, Missouri before she married. Of her three children, Harry received the largest amount of attention. From the start she and Harry shared a special closeness that made everyone accept him as mama's boy.

Although his mother was in no hurry to send Harry off to school, she took an early interest in his education. By the age of five Harry could read with speed and precision the large print of the big family bible. However, he was unable to read the smaller print in the newspaper. Harry's mother took him to the doctor, who diagnosed him with *hyperopia*, a condition where one's eyeballs are unnaturally flat. At age six Harry started to wear glasses with extremely thick corrective lenses, and in those days any child with eyeglasses was a curiosity.

Because of his glasses Harry was under strict orders not to rough-house or take part in contact sports. He volunteered to umpire baseball games rather than take his turn at bat, and that way Harry managed to remain a vital part of the fun without risking damage to his glasses. This sacrifice was not as big for Harry as it might have been for other boys. He could read all he wished, and books always offered him access to new worlds of action and adventure. Besides the bible, Harry loved to read biographies and history books. His favorite set of books was the series his mother bought him: *Great Men and Famous Women.* By the time he was thirteen, Harry had read nearly every book in the public library in Independence, Missouri.

Despite his efforts to make friends, Harry discovered that there were many who did not appreciate an undersized boy with oversized glasses. Those who considered themselves the tough members of the community regarded anyone who spent as much time as he did, with his face buried in books, with suspicion, even contempt.

He never got into a fistfight, but "sissy" was a name he heard more than once. "Little sissy Truman!" The name hurt. It had to. But Harry gritted his teeth and refused to be drawn into an open fight. Often he recalled his mother's words, "fighting is for babies," which helped him turn away from physical encounters. "If there was any danger of getting into a fight," he said, "I always ran." He became a member of the Waldo Street gang in Independence, Missouri, but he still managed to stay out of trouble.

Harry enjoyed listening to his mother play the piano and jumped at the chance to take lessons when she suggested it. Once again he ignored the taunts and jeers of those who thought music lessons were for sissies, listening only to the sounds he made as his hands flew gracefully over the keyboard.

He helped his mother in the kitchen and cared for his baby sister, braiding her hair and singing her to sleep. An accident-prone youngster, he once broke his collarbone in a fall from a chair while combing his hair. He nearly choked to death on a peach pit, but his mother was able to force the seed down his throat with her fingers. Harry also slammed the cellar door on his left foot, shearing off the tip of his big toe. A doctor reattached it successfully.

Harry's bond with his mother deepened even further when a severe bout of diphtheria, an infectious disease of the throat, paralyzed his arms and legs when he was only nine-years-old. He spent seven months at home recuperating, watching his mother cook, sew and clean. Going outdoors was only possible when his father could wheel him around the neighborhood in a baby buggy. Slowly Harry recovered, due largely to his father and mother building his confidence while exercising his body each day. "He's a fighter!" his proud father told everyone, once his son regained his health.

In his final year of high school Harry helped start a school newspaper. It gave him an opportunity to express his ideas on international, national, and school events, as well as gather facts for news stories. This experience made him think about a future in journalism. "One who can use words well can communicate ideas and arouse emotions," Harry once wrote in the school paper. "Certainly, one must appreciate the great responsibility in accepting such a task."

In 1901, at the age of seventeen, Harry graduated from high school. The valedictorian of his class was his best friend, Charlie Ross, who eventually became Truman's press secretary when he was president. Truman's father's financial difficulties around the turn of the century made it impossible for Harry to enter college, and his poor eyesight prevented his admission to the U.S. Military Academy at West Point.

Meanwhile, Harry had become an accomplished pianist. In 1900, at age sixteen, his music teacher introduced him to the world-famous composer Ignace Paderewski, who happened to be in Kansas City on a tour. Paderewski gave young Truman a spot lesson on how to play his famed *Minuet in G*. Harry's teacher encouraged him to pursue a musical career, but when his father lost the family's money speculating in the stock market, he dropped his lessons and any plans for college, and went to work as a timekeeper for a railroad contractor. Until the outbreak of World War I, Truman worked first at a series of clerical jobs, most of which were in Kansas City, and then returned to his parents' farm outside Independence, where he remained for the next eleven years.

Harry joined the National Guard in 1905, at the age of twenty-one. In August of 1917, at age thirty-three, his unit was mobilized and he volunteered to serve in France as an artillery officer. Truman was on horseback when his artillery battery came under German fire. His horse was hit by shrapnel and fell into a shell hole, trapping Truman underneath – he had to be pulled from beneath the horse. About this time, several of the men in his unit broke ranks and ran.

Truman rallied the remainder with some harsh language he had learned while working on the Santa Fe railroad. The troops were so shocked to hear such language from Truman that they swung into action immediately.

Harry was discharged as a major in May, 1919, when he was thirty-five-years-old. Because Truman had no definite future, he had been reluctant to marry. Seven weeks after being released from the army, with their future uncertain, Harry married his childhood sweetheart, Elizabeth "Bess" Virginia Wallace, who was a year younger than he.

For a few years Truman was part owner of a haberdashery, a men's clothing store. He not only failed in this business, but he spent the next twelve years paying off a twenty-five thousand dollar debt. Because of his sense of integrity, he refused to file for bankruptcy.

At the age of thirty-eight Harry was catapulted onto the political scene by the Democratic political machine run by Thomas J. Pendergast. Truman was twice elected judge of the Eastern District of Jackson County – a non-judicial administrative position much like a county executive. During his first term, when Harry was forty-years-old, he decided to improve his education by attending night classes at the Kansas City Law School. However, he never received a law degree.

Truman was defeated for re-election to a third term as judge largely because of the opposition of the Ku Klux Klan, which mistakenly believed he was part Jewish because one of his grandfathers was named Solomon Young. Eventually he was elected as a presiding judge, even though he had never taken the bar exam, and he held this office for eight years. He went on to become a United States Senator for two terms, before becoming vice president under President Franklin Delano Roosevelt. Four months into an unprecedented fourth term, President Roosevelt died, and Harry Truman became the thirty-third President of the United States.

More Information About Harry S Truman

State Represented	Missouri
Party Affiliation	Democrat
Siblings	First of Three Children
School(s) Attended	Kansas City Law School
Occupation(s)	Lawyer
Hobbies	Reading, Piano, Swimming, Wrestling
Political Particulars In Office	Bombing of Hiroshima & Nagasaki; Truman Doctrine; North Atlantic Treaty Organization; The Fair Deal; Korean War
States in Union During Teenage Years	Forty-five

DWIGHT DAVID EISENHOWER

Thirty-Fourth President of the United States
Lived: 1890 – 1969   Served: 1953 – 1961

Of all the previous presidents, Dwight D. Eisenhower had the most in common with Ulysses S. Grant, the seventeenth President of the United States. Eisenhower and Grant are, thus far, the only two West Point graduates to become president. Both had been commanding generals of victorious armies, and neither had any prior political experience or had ever been elected to another public office.

Dwight, the third of seven sons, was born in Denison, Texas. When he was still an infant, his family moved to Abilene, Kansas, after his father's work as the manager of a general store proved unsuccessful. In Abilene, Dwight's father became a hardworking mechanic in a creamery. Both his parents were members of a Protestant sect called the *River Brethren*, and his mother was a member of the Jehovah Witnesses. The children were brought up in an old-fashioned atmosphere of puritanical morals, and the influence of religion was paramount in every sphere of their lives. It extended from family prayers and communal bible study, to school and Sunday school. Violence was forbidden, although in a family of all boys, the edict was tough to enforce.

Dwight grew up in a family poorer than most in Abilene. With many mouths to feed and little income, the Eisenhowers struggled to make ends meet. As soon as each boy became old enough, he worked in the family garden to help grow vegetables for the table. To earn spare cash Dwight peddled produce from the family garden, and when he got a little older he worked doing various odd jobs. Dwight worked in the local creamery after school, and on vacations he hauled ice and shoveled snow.

Eisenhower lived in the poorer section of town where there were no sewers or paved roads. There was a traditional rivalry between the boys who lived on the two sides of the Union Pacific railroad tracks in Abilene, and every year a representative from each side met in a fistfight. When Dwight was fifteen, he got into one of these fights. The other boy was by far bigger and quicker, and the town's boys believed that Dwight would be knocked out in no time at all. After two full hours of fighting, the other boy announced that he could not beat Dwight.

A few months later Dwight fell and skinned his knee. He developed blood poisoning, and it spread through his entire leg. The doctor insisted that amputation was necessary. Dwight told his brothers to stand guard at his bed to prevent the doctor from operating: "You've got to promise me you won't let 'em do it," he sobbed. "You got to promise. I won't be a cripple. I'd rather die." When the infection subsided, the lesson was not lost on Dwight. Sheer will is a strong weapon.

Dwight was permitted considerable freedom as a boy, but it was limited by the authority of his devout parents. Dwight later described his father not only as the breadwinner, but also as Supreme Court and Lord High Executioner. His father worked twelve hours a day at the creamery, imposed a rigid discipline on the household, and punished without mercy those who misbehaved.

Dwight was often beaten for climbing onto the roof of the barn. The boys usually took their "lickings" like men, and as men, believed that such treatment had been good for them as boys. But Dwight did once try to physically restrain his father from thrashing Edgar, his older brother, exclaiming, "I don't think anyone ought to be whipped like that, not even a dog."

Eisenhower's mother taught her boys the bible, and she gave Dwight a gold watch for reading it from start to finish. She also distributed the chores – cooking, cleaning, washing, chopping wood, feeding the pigs and poultry, milking the cows, tending the crops, storing the produce, curing meat in the smokehouse – and she rotated the tasks among her sons in order to reduce the boredom.

Dwight's mother dressed her boys in such motley and threadbare clothing that the younger ones had to wear their mother's old button-top shoes to school. It made them a laughing stock. "Ridicule in turn," said Edgar, "made us scrappers." Young Dwight was a typical product of a lackluster environment. All accounts of his childhood confirm how ordinary he was. Many anecdotes sustain the view that he was just another noisy, mischievous, inquisitive, good-hearted, grinning boy.

Dwight took a variety of standard part-time jobs growing up. At age seven he earned a nickel a day delivering newspapers. Dwight was more interested in the backwoods than in his books. Indeed, his education, first in elementary school and then in high school, was meager. In high school his favorite subjects were history and plane geometry. His logical mind and excellent memory enabled him to get maximum grades with minimum effort. Eisenhower organized the high school athletic association and played baseball and football. He also played Shylock's servant in a senior class spoof of William Shakespeare's play *A Merchant of Venice*. A local reviewer wrote, "He was the best amateur, humorous character seen on the Abilene stage in this generation."

In 1909, Dwight's older brother Edgar went to study law at the University of Michigan. His father would not support him because he considered the field of law a wretched profession, so Dwight agreed to assist Edgar instead. The understanding was that this help would be reciprocated the following year, when Edgar would earn money and Dwight would enter the University of Michigan. So Dwight took a job in the creamery, rising from iceman to stoker, and then to night foreman. Much of Dwight's ninety dollars a month went to Edgar.

The Eisenhowers could not afford to send Dwight to college. It was only after a close friend suggested that Dwight go to the U.S. Naval Academy in Annapolis, Maryland that he decided not to follow his brother to Michigan. Attracted by the opportunity for a free college education, Eisenhower took the entrance examination for the Naval Academy but was informed that, having passed his twentieth birthday, he was too old for admission. The entrance exam was the same for both the Naval Academy and the U.S. Military Academy at West Point. He passed with flying colors, and was jubilant when the senator from Kansas appointed him to West Point.

Dwight's decision to attend West Point was quite accidental and had nothing to do with any military ambitions. In fact, he was not principally concerned with preparing himself for a career, but he wanted to complete his education, which to him meant playing football in college.

The new gym at West Point symbolized the importance of athletic pursuits in 1910. Dwight thrived in this atmosphere, and did well in many sports – boxing, baseball, running and gymnastics. But he chiefly distinguished himself in an institution obsessed with football; he played, worked, talked, thought and dreamed football. He even ate football, stuffing himself with food to increase his weight.

In his freshman year Dwight earned a place on the junior football squad, and in the autumn of 1912 his dream came true when he was promoted to West Point's varsity team. Within a few weeks the New York Times hailed him as "one of the most promising backs in Eastern football." By his second year he was well on his way to becoming a star halfback. But in a game against Tufts University, Eisenhower injured his knee so badly that he was barred permanently from ever playing football again. He grew despondent and even considered dropping out of the Academy; the only reason he stayed was to coach the junior varsity squad.

After four years at West Point, Eisenhower graduated ninety-fifth out of one hundred and sixty four students in overall conduct. He received demerits for various minor infractions, such as smoking or tardiness. He was once downgraded from sergeant to private for ignoring a warning to refrain from whirling his partner so vigorously around the ballroom in a dance class. Eisenhower blamed his behavior on a lack of interest in anything but athletics. In academic performance Dwight graduated sixty-first in his class. His best subjects were engineering, ordinance, gunnery and drill regulation. Soon after his graduation he went to the U.S. Army War College, where he graduated first out of two hundred and seventy five officers.

After leaving West Point, Dwight remained in the army, rising from second lieutenant to become a Five Star General and a hero during World War II. He served as supreme commander of the troops invading France on D-Day in 1944. Eisenhower spent eleven years of his army career with the rank of major, serving as a coach for the army football team.

After retiring from the army, Dwight became president of Columbia University, and then took leave to assume supreme command over the new NATO forces being assembled in 1951. In 1952 Eisenhower, somewhat reluctantly, became the Republican nominee for president. "I like Ike" (his nickname) proved to be an irresistible slogan, and he went on to win election over the Democratic candidate Adlai Stevenson by a tremendous margin. He served two terms in office, and by the time he left the White House at the age of seventy, Dwight Eisenhower was the oldest man to have served as the United States President (a record not broken until President Ronald Reagan was elected in 1981).

More Information About Dwight D. Eisenhower	
Born & Lived	b. Texas; l. Kansas
State Represented	New York
Party Affiliation	Republican
Siblings	Third of Seven Children
School(s) Attended	U.S. Military Academy at West Point, Army War College
Occupation(s)	Army Officer; University President
Hobbies	Football, baseball, boxing, gymnastics, running, fishing, golfing, bridge
Political Particulars in Office	Obtained truce with Korea in 1953; Championed construction of Interstate Highway System; Eisenhower Doctrine to end the Suez Crisis; Tried to ease tensions of the Cold War
States in Union During Teenage Years	Forty-six

JOHN FITZGERALD KENNEDY

Thirty-Fifth President of the United States
Lived: 1917 – 1963   Served: 1961 – 1963

As the first Roman Catholic to become president, John (Jack) F. Kennedy won out over the religious bigotry that had helped defeat Al Smith, four-term Governor of New York, thirty years earlier. His election over Republican Vice President Richard Nixon was also hailed as a triumph for the modern communication marvel of television. Kennedy overshadowed his better-known opponent in a series of televised debates during the political campaign. Even so, Kennedy's plurality was the smallest in history – only two-tenths of a percent of the popular vote. John F. Kennedy was the fourth president to be assassinated in office.

Jack Kennedy, the second of nine children, was born at home in Brookline, Massachusetts. The United States entered World War I one month before he was born. Kennedy was the first president born in the twentieth century. Jack had five sisters and three brothers, two of whom also ran for president (Robert in 1968, Edward in 1972 and 1980). His sister Rosemary was born mentally handicapped.

Both of Jack's parents came from a long line of political figures. His father, Joseph P. Kennedy, was a very wealthy man who earned his fortune in banking, finance, and real estate – he was a millionaire by the time he was thirty-five. He was appointed U.S. Ambassador to Great Britain by President Franklin Roosevelt prior to World War II.

Jack's mother, Rose Kennedy, was educated at convent schools in Boston and in the Netherlands. She also studied piano at the New England Conservatory of Music. Her father had been mayor of Boston from 1906-1907 and 1910-1914.

The Kennedy's moved often, to bigger homes and better neighborhoods, as the family grew and Joseph Kennedy became wealthier. Jack attributed much of his success to his father. "My father," President Kennedy once said, "wasn't around as much as some fathers when I was young; but whether he was there or not, he made his children feel that they were the most important things in the world to him."

Jack's father was very strict. He liked his boys to win at sports and everything they tried. If they didn't win, he discussed their failures with them, but he did not have much patience with the loser. Victory and courage were the keystones of their father's philosophy, and he tried to pass that along to all his children. He tried to instill in them a fierce competitive spirit, firm discipline, and a compelling drive to win.

Although Kennedy's father was very wealthy, money was rarely used as a reward. Jack's father exacted a firm pledge from each of his children not to smoke or drink until he or she reached the age of twenty-one. Their incentive for keeping this promise was a bonus of $2,000, payable on their twenty-first birthdays. What was kept a secret was that a trust fund of one million dollars had been generated for each child, which s/he would receive when s/he turned twenty-one. Jack's father was adamant that his children should be financially independent and have the courage to make up their own minds.

Jack was a sickly child. He contracted scarlet fever when he was only two-years-old and almost died. He spent much of his childhood recuperating from a host of other ailments, including whooping cough, measles, chicken pox, bronchitis, tonsillitis, appendicitis, and jaundice. Most of his life he had problems with his back. His brothers used to joke that Jack was so sickly that a mosquito took a big risk in biting him. Still, he was an active child, a scrapper who took a lot of pounding from his older brother Joe.

When it came to his education, Jack learned the fundamentals at public schools in Massachusetts and New York. Jack loved to read; his mother remembered that she rarely saw Jack by himself without a book. Nothing made him happier than being the first to get the newspaper each day. He read with such complete concentration that he noticed nothing else going on around him. His reading habits, and his passion for reading, remained with him throughout his life.

When Jack was thirteen-years-old he studied at the Canterberry Catholic School in Connecticut, until an attack of appendicitis forced his withdrawal. He then spent four years at Choate, a private preparatory school where he showed signs of promise, but was more interested in pranks than study. "Jack has a clever, individual mind," reported his headmaster. "When he learns the right place for humor, and learns to use his individual way of looking at things as an asset instead of a handicap, his natural gift of an individual outlook and witty expression are going to help him." At Choate, Jack was nicknamed "rat face" for his scrawny appearance. At the time he was all of six feet tall and weighed one hundred and thirty five pounds. Jack graduated a lackluster sixty-fourth out of one hundred and twelve students, but was voted "most likely to succeed."

Kennedy's main failings were scholastic. His grades were well above average in English and history, but he had trouble with foreign languages, especially Latin. Biology and chemistry bored him. Consequently, he found himself in trouble several times. He was aware that his father wanted him to do well, and he worked hard when the subject matter interested him, but he found it difficult to sit down and apply himself in courses that didn't interest him. Despite problems with his grades, Jack kept abreast of current events. He wrote to his father asking him to send the *Literary Digest*, a political magazine from the early 1930's.

During the summer of 1935, at age eighteen, Jack studied at the London School of Economics. While there he became ill with jaundice and had to withdraw. The following fall he enrolled at Princeton University, but a recurrence of jaundice forced his withdrawal once again. He then decided to attend Harvard University, his father's alma mater. There he majored in political science, with an emphasis on international relations. Until that point he was barely keeping a C grade point average, and it was not until his junior year that he began to take his studies seriously.

In 1939, at the end of his sophomore year, at age twenty-two, Kennedy toured Europe and then spent the second semester of his junior year working as secretary to his father who, at that time, was serving as the U.S. Ambassador to Great Britain. Hitler was already waging war in Europe and, traveling from country to country, Jack was able to interview politicians and statesmen. He sent his father detailed reports of the crisis that led up to World War II. Back at Harvard, Kennedy tried to explain in his senior thesis why Britain had not been ready for war. His thesis, published as *Why England Slept*, became a best-selling book.

In extracurricular activities, Kennedy played end on the freshman and junior varsity football teams, and held a place on the 1938 championship sailing crew. He was also on the freshman swim and golf teams and took part in intramural softball and hockey. He was on the staff of the *Harvard Crimson* newspaper and a member of the Hasty Pudding Club, a theatrical group. Mainly because of his senior honors thesis, *Why England Slept,* Kennedy graduated cum laude in political science at the age of twenty-three. He studied briefly at Stanford Business School before touring South America.

When the United States declared war on Japan on December 7, 1941, Jack's brother Joseph Jr. enlisted in the air force. Jack also tried to enlist, but was rejected because of his bad back. He then tried to volunteer for the army, and again was rejected because of his back. After taking a strenuous course of exercises, he passed the navy physical examination and was accepted as a seaman at age twenty-four. After spending over a year at various desk jobs, Jack asked his father to use his influence to get him sea duty. He soon was assigned to PT-boat (patrol torpedo) training. He received a commission as a lieutenant junior grade, and in March, 1943, was given his own torpedo boat (PT-109) in the South Pacific.

After a Japanese destroyer sliced through his torpedo boat, Jack struggled to stay alive and two of his crew died. Despite his weak back, Kennedy not only managed to swim four hours to safety, but he also towed an injured crewman by the life jacket strap with his teeth. For his bravery and courage he received the Purple Heart, and the Navy and Marine Corps Medal. Because of his injuries Kennedy was discharged from the navy in 1945, just before the end of World War II.

Following his discharge from the navy, Jack worked briefly as a journalist for the Chicago Herald and the International News Service. With a little prodding from his father, he decided to run for his first public office as a U.S. Representative at the age of twenty-eight. After being elected as a congressman three times, he was elected as a U.S. Senator from Massachusetts for two six-year terms.

During his second term in congress, Senator Kennedy had his second spinal surgery. He had unsuccessful back surgery in 1944 because of the injuries sustained during the sinking of the PT-boat. During his long months of convalescence Kennedy wrote *Profiles of Courage*, for which he was awarded the Pulitzer Prize. In 1960, at the age of forty-three, John F. Kennedy became the youngest man ever elected president. In his Inaugural Address he called on all citizens to "Ask not what your country can do for you, ask what you can do for your country."

President John F. Kennedy was assassinated by the gunman Lee Harvey Oswald on November 22, 1963.

More Information About John F. Kennedy	
State Represented	Massachusetts
Party Affiliation	Democrat
Siblings	Second of Nine Children
Pet(s)	Ponies
School(s) Attended	Harvard University
Occupation(s)	Journalist, Author, Secretary to U.S. Ambassador to Great Britain
Hobbies	Swimming, football, sailing, golfing, softball, hockey, reading, current events
Political Particulars in Office	Bay of Pigs invasion of Cuba in 1961 (attempt to overthrow government of Fidel Castro); Cuban Missile Crisis; saw building of Berlin Wall; supported Space Race; Civil Rights advocate; Created Peace Corps
States in Union During Teenage Years	Forty-eight

LYNDON BAINES JOHNSON

Thirty-Sixth President of the United States
Lived: 1908 – 1973   Served: 1963 – 1969

Lyndon Johnson was the eighth vice president to become chief executive after a president died in office. He aspired to be president while he was still in high school.

Lyndon was born in a three-room farmhouse in the bleak hill-country near Stonewall, Texas. The oldest of five children, Lyndon had three sisters and a brother. The Johnsons were not poor, but they knew hard times and labored for what they earned.

Johnson's father was a high school graduate and taught school before becoming a farmer. Lyndon's mother graduated from college and worked as a teacher. She taught oratory for a time before getting married, and she edited a small local newspaper.

With his mother's coaching, Lyndon learned the alphabet at age two and was reading by the age of four. He attended public elementary schools near Stonewall and in Johnson City, Texas, a city which his family had helped settle. Although he was bright, Lyndon disliked homework, especially math, and was often cited for misbehaving.

Lyndon studied violin for several months, and his mother thought it would be a good idea to send her boy to dance classes where he could meet other children his age and make friends. He teased the other children and tormented the girls by slyly putting pebbles or grains of wheat into their dancing shoes.

When Lyndon was nine-years-old, he became a shoeshine boy to make some extra money. He did this in addition to doing his household chores and looking after his younger brother and sisters. During summer vacations young Lyndon took a job as a goat herder – it was an opportunity to show his fearlessness and independence, and a chance to build self-confidence. Lyndon also worked in the cotton fields that his uncle owned.

Early in 1918, when Lyndon was only ten-years-old, his dad was elected to fill an unexpired term as a representative to the Texas State Legislature. Lyndon was very excited about his father's campaign and liked to accompany him on his trips. Lyndon helped milk the cows and feed the other farm animals before joining his father on the campaign trail.

Lyndon graduated from the seventh grade of his one-room schoolhouse in the spring of 1920, when he was eleven-years-old. The following spring he graduated from the eighth grade of an elementary school in the village of Stonewall. That fall, at age thirteen, he arranged to attend a three-year high school.

In order to get to and from the high school, Lyndon had to ride eight miles each way by horseback, and he loved the rides. In high school Lyndon had trouble keeping busy. He learned his lessons readily and was eager to do extra reading, but he found few suitable books in the school library. His chief recreation was playing baseball with the other boys at recess. One recess after he finished playing baseball, he sat down under a tree to rest. A classmate, Anna Itz, sat nearby, but neither spoke. Suddenly Lyndon broke the silence: "Someday I am going to be the President of the United States."

While Lyndon was only fourteen, he was proud of his father who was helping pass laws that were good for the people. Lyndon frequently attended sessions of the state legislature and followed the debate. When there was no room to sit, he stood and listened carefully so he could learn and take it all in.

Lyndon fondly recalled a thrilling childhood trip to the Alamo with his father. He was deeply moved by the valor of Jim Bowie and Davy Crockett and the others who died defending the mission. The many pictures and maps on the walls helped him imagine the details of the massacre.

During Lyndon's second year of high school his father suffered serious financial problems, and once again they were going to have to move. This time from the farm back to the city, but Lyndon had no problem adjusting. As a senior, he became class president. He was also a member of the baseball and debate teams. Outside of school Lyndon found jobs to help make ends meet. He returned to working as a shoeshine boy. When Lyndon graduated from Johnson City High School the following spring, he was only sixteen-years-old. At the graduation exercises he read the class poem, gave the class prophecy, and delivered the valedictory address. After graduation he had to get a job, because his father could not afford to send him to college.

Lyndon decided to go to California to look for work. His father bitterly opposed the idea of Lyndon making such a trip because he was so young, but six boys pooled their money and bought an old Model-T Ford to head west. Their trip was much slower and harder than they had anticipated. All they had to eat were the slices of fat-back (un-smoked salt pork) and cornbread with molasses they had brought from home. Each night they slept on the ground next to the road. During the latter part of the trip they ran out of both food and money. Without money they could purchase neither gasoline for their car nor food to fill their stomachs, so they had to stop along the way and work odd jobs to earn money before they could go on.

Once in California Lyndon still couldn't find employment, but he was determined. He hitchhiked and tramped up and down the coast, working on farms, cultivating gardens, waiting tables, washing dishes, working any job he could find. At night, if he was working in the country he slept outdoors, and if he was working in the city he slept in a cheap rooming house.

After eighteen months in California, Lyndon decided to return to Texas. He had so little money that he hitchhiked all the way home to Johnson City. His parents encouraged him to go to college, but he was stubborn and just wanted to find a job.

During the next few months he worked several low paying jobs in and around Johnson City. Finally his father, who was the foreman of a road gang, gave him a job that paid a dollar a day. Lyndon drove a truck, pushed a wheelbarrow, and shoveled gravel and dirt. He had to work outdoors in all kinds of weather, from scorching heat to pene-trating cold. Often he got caught in the rain with no means of protec-tion. One rain-swept morning in February, 1927, he suddenly dashed into the house and announced, "Mama, if you and Papa can get me in, I'm ready to go to college."

A short time after he enrolled in Southwest Texas State Teachers' College at San Marcos, Lyndon decided he should get a job using his head instead of his hands. He walked into the college president's office and requested a job working for him. The president told Lyndon that he already had a secretary and didn't need anyone else, but Lyndon was so persistent that the president finally gave him a job as an assistant to the secretary, to work during his free time between classes.

Johnson was behind in the required courses in college because he came from a three-year high school, and he had to make up for lost time. He was such a brilliant student, however, that he completed the necessary coursework in a few months and became a full-fledged college student. He majored in history and studied other social sciences, and he got such high grades in those courses that he was invited to join the National Social Science Honor Society.

In addition to taking a full load of college courses and working to earn a living, he took part in many activities. As a freshman, he wrote a weekly article for the college newspaper, and a year later he became the editor.

At the peak of Lyndon's college career he suffered a serious interruption. His father's financial situation worsened and Lyndon had to help support his family. He got a job teaching, and at the same time he took several more courses to speed up his graduation date. His last year of college was a huge success. He joined the debate team and was one of the most successful debaters the college ever had. He was a member and leader of almost every student organization on campus.

While in college Lyndon was informally engaged to the daughter of a prominent Ku Klux Klan leader in Texas. Under severe pressure from his father, who was adamantly opposed to the KKK, Lyndon broke off the engagement.

Lyndon Johnson went on to work as a teacher and debate coach at Sam Houston High School in Houston, Texas. His team won both the city championship and the regional state championship. Lyndon married Claudia Alta "Lady Bird" Taylor, when he was twenty-six and she was twenty-one. It was at this time, in 1934, that Johnson began studying law at Georgetown Law School, although he dropped out before years end.

He served two years in the U.S. Navy as a lieutenant commander, and was awarded the Silver Star after being attacked by Japanese aircraft while on a special mission.

Johnson quit the field of education and became heavily involved in politics. He served six terms as a U.S. Congressman and two terms as a U.S. Senator. At age forty-six he became the youngest majority leader in Senate history. After becoming vice president in 1960, Lyndon Baines Johnson became President of the United States upon the assassination of President John F. Kennedy in 1963. In 1964 Lyndon Johnson won the presidential election with the widest popular margin in American history.

More Information About Lyndon B. Johnson

State Represented	Texas
Party Affiliation	Democrat
Siblings	First of Five Children
Pet(s)	Dogs: Beagles named *Him* and *Her*
School(s) Attended	Southwest Texas State Teachers' College
Occupation(s)	Teacher, Debate Coach, Rancher
Hobbies	Horseback Riding, Baseball, Reading, Debating, Hunting, Fishing,
Political Particulars in Office	"A Great Society" – passed one of the most extensive legislative programs in the nation's history, improving education, conservation, urban renewal; Passed Medicare amendment to Social Security Act; Vietnam War
States in Union During Teenage Years	Forty-eight

RICHARD MILHOUS NIXON

Thirty-Seventh President of the United States
Lived 1913 – 1994 Served 1969 – 1974

Richard Nixon had no famous ancestors, nor any relatives who were rich. There was not a political leader in his family. Nixon is the only person to have been elected twice to the vice presidency and twice to the presidency. He was also the first president to resign from office; because of scandal, he was facing impeachment and conviction before he completed his second term in office.

Richard was born on a lemon farm in Yorba Linda, California, in a small frame-house his father built. Nixon's parents lived on the edge of poverty for the first nine years of their marriage. Richard was the second of five sons, two of whom died of tuberculosis – one at age seven and the other at twenty-three. Both proved to be very traumatic experiences for Nixon.

Richard's father, Frank Nixon, never finished high school. He dropped out of grade school to work as a farmhand, and then as a house painter, a telephone lineman and several other jobs. He later became a gas station owner and grocer. Richard's mother was raised as an evangelical Quaker, and was a student at Whittier College in California when she met Frank. Her ambition for her son was for him to become a Quaker missionary.

Religion, family, and school were the center of Nixon's life. There were daily prayers, and church services of one kind or another, four times on Sunday. There he learned tolerance and the Quaker distaste for showing emotion. He learned to love poetry and to recite it before an audience, and he learned modesty in all things.

At age three Richard fell out of a buggy and gashed his scalp on the wagon wheel. He nearly bled to death during the twenty-five mile trip to the nearest hospital. At age four he again almost died, this time from pneumonia. When he was well he was a quiet, obedient child, dutifully helping out with chores and keeping out of mischief.

He grew up in an atmosphere of security, surrounded by love. Richard turned instinctively to his mother for comfort; he liked to have her sit with him while he read. His father sometimes frightened him, but he never had cause to doubt his father's love or protection. Richard worked hard, not only in his studies, but also in the lemon groves. He had to hoe weeds for his father and help with the irrigation.

As a youngster, Nixon loved to escape the real world by daydreaming and reading. His mother taught him to read when he was five, and it wasn't long before he was reading everything he could get his hands on. Richard acquired the nickname "Gloomy Gus," because it seemed that his nose was always stuck in a book. His father could holler all he wanted, but if Richard had a book he would be out reading in a corner or behind the shed or anywhere his father couldn't find him.

Richard was very mature, even as a young child. He was interested in things beyond the grasp of a typical boy his age. He rarely traveled – he never went up to the mountains, and only once or twice did he go to the ocean. He had no hobbies, not even hunting and fishing, which were so common among rural boys. Instead he did most of his traveling in his mind. He borrowed magazines and books from his grandmother, his aunt and other relatives – *National Geographic* magazine was his favorite. He was thoughtful and serious, and he absorbed knowledge of every kind. He read no less than thirty or forty books a year, besides doing all his other work. Nixon's excellent memory helped him store everything he read.

Richard's father was passionate about politics. The other boys were not much interested, but Richard was fascinated. By age six he was reading the front page of the newspaper and discussing public events with his father. When the Teapot Dome scandal (fraud and corruption during President Harding's Administration) broke in 1924, his father denounced the corrupt politicians and the high-priced lawyers who defended them. "When I get big, I'll be a lawyer they can't bribe," Richard said.

Presidents Were Teenagers Too

In grade school Nixon participated in schoolyard baseball and football games. Because his coordination was poor, and he was below average in size, he did not stand out. His talent was in music — at age seven he began taking piano and violin lessons.

Richard was a boy who attacked with words rather than fists. His talents were mental, not physical. He could never beat his older brother Harold, or his cousin Floyd, or almost anyone else in sports competition, but he beat them all as a speaker and as a student. He enjoyed public speaking and was good at it. He responded well to an audience, speaking with confidence and skill. People were amazed by his ability to memorize, by the interest he took in national politics and his knowledge about public issues. Nearly everyone who knew him remarked on his serious nature, his competitiveness and his ambition.

Richard had a vivid imagination and an impressive ability as a writer when he was only ten-years-old. As a result of his bookworm habits, the long hours he spent at work, and his shyness and sense of unease with a friend or a small group, he was not very popular. "He was a little different than the rest of us," a classmate recalled.

One characteristic that bothered his classmates was Richard's love of argument. Like his father, he enjoyed it for its own sake, although he was more inclined to use logic and reason than the strength of his voice to make his points. Nixon did earn his classmate's respect, if not their love. He brought home mostly A grades, to his father's delight. Richard skipped second grade and was the valedictorian of his grammar school.

Richard's lack of popularity bothered him, and he compensated with aggressiveness. After his retirement he said, "What starts the process, really, are laughs and slights and snubs when you are a kid. But," he added, "if you are reasonably intelligent and if your anger is deep enough and strong enough, you learn that you can change those attitudes by excellence, personal gut performance, while those who have everything are sitting on their fat butts."

While in high school, and at his father's urging, he tried out for football, basketball and track. There were long hours of practice involved, much hard work, and much frustration. His favorite class in high school was debate. Between sports, schoolwork, study, the store, and church, he hardly had time to sleep. Richard kept up this brutal schedule through high school and into college.

As a senior in high school, Richard was a champion debater, had the lead role in the Latin play, was an honor student, and upon graduation was given the Harvard Club award for being the best all-around student. Nixon graduated from Whittier High first in his class of 1930, and was presented the California Interscholastic Federation Gold Seal Award for scholarship.

At age seventeen Nixon went to Whittier College instead of going to Harvard University, because his parents couldn't afford the expenses. Richard always claimed that it never made a difference to him where he went, as long as he went to college. During his four years at Whittier College he majored in history and was captain of the debate team. He also played second-string tackle on the football team and belonged to the drama and glee clubs. As a senior, he was elected president of the student body. He graduated from Whittier College second of eighty-five students in the class of 1934.

Richard applied for and received a scholarship to Duke University Law School. He and three other students shared a rundown off-campus farmhouse that had no running water or electricity. Once again he was elected president of his class. He graduated from Duke Law School third of twenty-five students in the class of 1937, and was admitted to the California Bar Association that same year.

In April of 1942, three months after Pearl Harbor was bombed by the Japanese, at the age of twenty-nine, Nixon joined the U.S. Navy. After spending four years in the navy, Nixon served in the House of Representatives for two terms before being elected to the U.S. Senate in 1950. Before his term was up in the Senate he became Dwight D. Eisenhower's vice presidential running mate in 1952, when he was thirty-nine-years-old. He served as vice president from 1953-1961, and then lost the presidential bid to John F. Kennedy in 1960. He then lost the election for the Governorship of California in 1962. Finally, in 1968, he ran and won the presidential election against Hubert Humphrey. During his second term in office, because of the Watergate scandal, his administration was embattled in scandal and Nixon decided to resign instead of going through impeachment proceedings.

More Information About Richard M. Nixon	
Born and Lived	California
State Represented	New York
Party Affiliation	Republican
Siblings	Second of Five Children
Pet(s)	Dogs: French Poodle named *Vicky*, Yorkshire Terrier named *Pasha*, Irish Setter named *King Timahoe*, Cocker Spaniel named *Checkers*
School(s) Attended	Whittier College, Duke University Law School
Occupation(s)	Lawyer
Hobbies	Reading, Debate, Piano, Violin, Baseball
Political Particulars in Office	Ended War in Vietnam; Reduced tensions with China and U.S.S.R; Astronauts made first moon landing in 1969; Created Environmental Protection Agency and Drug Enforcement Administration; Resigned because of Watergate scandal
States in Union During Teenage Years	Forty-eight

GERALD RUDOLPH FORD

Thirty-Eighth President of the United States

Lived 1913 – 2006   Served 1974 – 1977

Gerald R. Ford was the first man to occupy the White House without being elected either president or vice president. He was appointed vice president under the terms of the twenty-fifth amendment, and he became the only vice president in American history to succeed to the nation's highest office because of the resignation of a president. Both events resulted from two of the worst scandals in American political history: the forced resignation of Vice President Spiro Agnew after he pled guilty to a charge of income tax evasion, and the resignation of President Richard Nixon brought about by the Watergate scandal.

Dorothy Gardner was twenty-years-old in 1912 when she married Leslie Lynch King, a thirty-year-old wool merchant. He was a blond-haired, blue-eyed, charming son of a wealthy Omaha banker who owned a stagecoach line. On their honeymoon Dorothy discovered that she had made a terrible mistake. Her new husband struck her repeatedly, and when they reached Omaha, Nebraska, where they were to live with his family, she found out that King was not only brutal, but a liar and a drunk. His outward charm concealed a vicious temper. Dorothy planned to leave King, but discovered she was pregnant. With the encouragement of King's mother and father, she decided to have the baby in Omaha. The baby was named Leslie Lynch King, Jr., the name of his biological father.

A few days later Leslie King, Sr. entered his wife's room with a butcher knife and threatened to kill mother, child and nurse. Police were called to restrain him. Divorce was rare in 1913, but an Omaha court found King guilty of extreme cruelty, and two years later granted custody of the child to his mother and ordered King to pay alimony and child support. King refused to pay anything. Dorothy King and her son Leslie, Jr. moved to Grand Rapids, Michigan, to live with her parents.

By good fortune, in her son's first year Dorothy, who was now twenty-four-years-old, met a man whose character matched and complemented her own. He was a tall, dark-haired and amiable bachelor named Gerald Rudolf Ford who was twenty-six-years-old. By trade Ford was a paint salesman. In the community he was respected as honest and hardworking, kind and considerate, a man of integrity and character – everything Dorothy's first husband was not. The next year she married Gerald R. Ford, and he adopted her two-year-old son. At this time Leslie Lynch King, Jr. became Gerald Rudolph Ford, Jr., believing his stepfather was his true father.

Gerald had no full siblings. From his biological father's second marriage, he had a half brother and two half sisters, and from his mother's second marriage to Gerald, he had three half brothers. He grew up as the oldest of seven children.

Ford's mother was a strict disciplinarian. She resolved that her oldest son must learn to control the hot temper he had inherited from his biological father. When the boy raged in anger, she tried to reason with him, or she sent him to his room to cool off. During one particular episode she had young Jerry memorize Rudyard Kipling's poem, *If*. After that she made him recite it every time he lost his temper.

From age two Gerald grew up in modest circumstances in Grand Rapids, Michigan. He was a spirited, industrious and athletic youngster. He helped with chores, tended to the coal furnace, mowed the lawn, and washed clothes. He and his family vacationed at Ottawa Beach on Lake Michigan, and fished at the Little South Branch of the Pere Marquette River. As a teenager, Jerry drove a used Model-T Ford with a rumble seat, but one day he threw a blanket on the overhead engine and returned to find the car destroyed in flames.

Ford wasn't told that he was adopted until he was twelve-years-old. At age seventeen his biological father appeared for the first time, at the restaurant where Jerry worked. After a very brief and awkward discussion, Leslie King, Sr. gave Jerry twenty-five dollars and left in his brand new Lincoln. Jerry never saw him again, and the encounter left him shaken and in tears.

Jerry had a big problem in his early years at school – he was left-handed and the teachers forced him to use his right hand to write. He also had a stuttering problem, and all teachers did in those days was yell at kids for stuttering. Jerry became demoralized and started to withdraw. It seemed that the more he had difficulty writing right-handed, the worse his stuttering became. It wasn't until his parents sought help from a psychiatrist that his problems disappeared. Once his teachers were told to allow Jerry to write with his left hand, his stuttering stopped.

After completing elementary school, Ford attended Grand Rapids South High School. He was a good student who excelled in history and government, performed well in math and the sciences, but did poorly in Latin. At the end of his junior year he made the National Honor Society and ranked in the top five percent of his class. Ford was also an Eagle Scout in the Boy Scouts of America, and he held two part-time jobs, working at an amusement park and flipping burgers in a restaurant.

He usually wore a suit and tie, while his classmates dressed in more casual attire. Ford was not stuffy though, on the contrary, he was popular and well-liked. In a movie theater promotional contest he won his first trip to Washington, D.C., and the title of most popular high school senior.

Ford was a husky youth, and he excelled at football. He was a star center for the South High Trojans football team and was named to the all-city squad. Following his high school graduation in 1931, he entered the University of Michigan on a partial scholarship as a pre-law student majoring in economics and political science. Generally a B student, he earned A's in four courses – money and credit, European history from the decline of Rome to 1648, organized labor, and American government. He helped work his way through college bussing tables in the university hospital dining room and washing dishes at his fraternity house, Delta Kappa Epsilon.

Jerry was named outstanding freshman on the Michigan Wolverines football team, but played second string during his sophomore and junior years behind All-American center Chuck Bernard. As a senior, he was named most valuable player and played center in the 1935 College All-Stars game against the Chicago Bears. Both the Detroit Lions and Green Bay Packers offered him professional contracts, but he turned them down to study law.

At age twenty-two Jerry graduated in the top twenty-five percent of Michigan University's class of 1935. That year he was hired at a salary of $2,400 a year to be the assistant football coach and head boxing coach at Yale University. Among those he coached in football were future senators Robert Taft, Jr. of Ohio, and William Proxmire of Wisconsin. Ford intended to begin taking law courses immediately, but because of his full-time coaching schedule, Yale officials denied him admission.

During the summer of 1936 Jerry worked as a park ranger at Yellowstone National Park, feeding the bears and directing traffic. He also worked for a time as a male model.

After Ford's repeated applications, officials at Yale Law School reluctantly accepted him on a trial basis in 1938. He surprised them by maintaining a B average and ranking in the top third of his class, which included such future notables as Supreme Court Justice Potter Stewart, Secretary of State Cyrus Vance, and Peace Corps Director Sargent Shriver. Ford's best subject was legal ethics. In 1941, at age twenty-eight, Ford received his law degree and was admitted to the Michigan State Bar Association.

In 1942 Jerry enlisted in the U.S. Navy. He rose from ensign to lieutenant commander, and after serving for four years, he left the military to practice law. He joined the law firm of Butterfield, Keeney and Amberg in Grand Rapids, Michigan. In 1948, at age thirty-five, he married thirty-year-old Elizabeth Ann Bloomer.

A year later he was elected as a U.S. Congressman, he served as the house minority leader, and remained in that position until President Nixon appointed him vice president in 1973. The following year President Nixon resigned and Gerald Ford became the thirty-eighth President of the United States.

His first act as president was to grant former President Richard Nixon a full pardon, even though he was never convicted of any crime. Ford worked hard throughout his term in office to heal the nation after the scandals that had wreaked such havoc.

More Information About Gerald R. Ford	
Born	Nebraska
State Represented	Michigan
Party Affiliation	Republican
Siblings	First of Seven Children
Pet(s)	Dog: Golden Retriever named *Liberty*
School(s) Attended	University of Michigan, Yale University Law School
Occupation(s)	Lawyer, Assistant Football / Head Boxing Coach at Yale, Park Ranger, Model
Hobbies	Football, Baseball, Boxing, Eagle Scout
Political Particulars in Office	Granted full pardon to former President Richard Nixon; Survived two assassination attempts
States in Union During Teenage Years	Forty-eight

JAMES EARL CARTER, JR.

Thirty-Ninth President of the United States
Lived: 1924 –   Served: 1977 – 1981

Jimmy Carter was born, grew up and spent nine years of his adult life in Plains, Georgia. Although other U.S. Presidents have come from small towns, no one else spent so many adult years in such a setting. Carter's roots in Georgia were strong and deep. He is the first president from the deep south since Zachary Taylor, the nation's twelfth president in 1848. Carter was also the first president born in a hospital.

The future president began life in a rented house in Plains. When he was four, he and his parents and his little sister Gloria, born when he was two, moved to a larger house on a farm his father had bought before getting married. Jimmy was the oldest of four children, two of whom were girls. Billy Carter, his youngest brother, was born thirteen years after Jimmy. Jimmy had his biggest quarrels and fights with his sisters when he was a kid.

The person who had the strongest influence on Jimmy was his mother, Lillian. She had a good mind, a strong sense of humor, and an insatiable curiosity about the world. An avid reader, she wanted her children to love books too, so they would know about things that were beyond their immediate vision. She taught Jimmy to read by the time he was four-years-old. Lillian was a deeply compassionate person who cared greatly about other human beings. Jimmy's father, James Earl Carter, Sr., only went as far as the tenth grade in high school. He rarely read, but he did serve for many years on the County School Board, and was elected to the Georgia State Legislature.

James Earl Carter, Jr.

The Carters lived in a rural area where there was no electricity, no telephone, and no plumbing. On winter nights Jimmy fell asleep snuggled against warm bricks that were heated on the stove, wrapped and carried to his bed. For part of his childhood there was no running water in the house. Jimmy wore no shoes from April to October, and he only wore a shirt to church and school.

Chores of all kinds had to be done – wood needed to be chopped for the fireplace; kerosene lamps had to be filled nightly; and the yard around the house, which consisted of sand rather than grass, had to be constantly swept. The Carter family wasn't poor, but they certainly weren't rich. Farming had been their family's work for generations, and the Carters were known to be hard workers.

One chore that Jimmy hated was "mopping" cotton. First he put a mixture of molasses, arsenic, and water into a bucket. Then, dipping a small rag mop into the bucket, he had to spread its sticky contents onto each bud of cotton. The job was messy and exhausting, but it was necessary to get rid of boll weevils (insects) that killed the cotton. Swarms of flies, attracted to the molasses, bit Jimmy's arms and face, and by the end of the day his pants were covered with a syrupy mess. When he took off his jeans at the end of the day, he had to stand them up in his bedroom because they were too stiff to bend.

Segregation was part of the Southern culture when Jimmy was growing up. Most of the children in his neighborhood were African-Americans, and almost all of Jimmy's playmates were black. Together they built tree houses, rode horses, milked cows and ground sugarcane. They worked in the fields together, and hunted and fished and swam together, but when it came time for church and school they went their separate ways without really understanding why.

At age five Jimmy sold boiled peanuts on the streets of Plains and helped work in the fields, but he still occasionally got into trouble because he was an adventurous and mischievous youngster. He later recalled that between the ages of four and fifteen he was whipped six times by his father – once for stealing a penny from the church collection plate, and another time for shooting his sister with a BB gun. Whippings were done with a small, long, flexible peach tree switch. Jimmy recalls these experiences vividly in his autobiography, *Why Not the Best?*

While still young, Jimmy was influenced by his mother's younger brother, Thomas Watson Gordy, who was a navy radioman. At age six Jimmy knew he wanted to join the United States Navy, and in the fourth grade he began checking out books from the library about the world's oceans. Before entering high school in the autumn of 1938, he wrote a letter to the U.S. Naval Academy in Annapolis, Maryland, asking for information about entrance requirements.

Jimmy's father had been a naval officer in World War I, so he was pleased when his son decided he wanted to enter the Naval Academy. Because it took a recommendation from a Congressman to get into Annapolis, Jimmy's father started to build a relationship with Stephen Pace, their Congressman from Georgia, and began contributing money to his campaigns.

Knowing he was at a disadvantage at Plains High School because they didn't have a full science curriculum, Jimmy spent many hours trying to teach himself. Jimmy loved to read and he got good grades in school — his favorite subjects were history and literature. He credited his high school teacher, Miss Julia Coleman, for playing an important role in shaping his life. "She saw something in me, I think, a hunger to learn." She encouraged his interest in literature, drew up reading lists for him and, when he was twelve, introduced him to *War and Peace* by Leo Tolstoy, a work that Jimmy was disappointed to learn was not about cowboys and Indians. President Carter paid tribute to Miss Coleman in his Inaugural Address.

Jimmy was an average athlete who did well on the track team, and even though he was small, he played on the high school basketball team. Most of all he liked the recreational pastimes of his childhood: hiking, bicycling, playing tennis, cross-country, skiing, and bowling. After high school he spent time with his father hunting.

Jimmy learned to speed read, and was clocked at 2,000 words per minute with a ninety-five percent comprehension rate.

Jimmy graduated from high school at age sixteen and was named valedictorian of his class. After high school, in 1942, Jimmy went to a small community college in Americus, Georgia. The country had just entered World War II, and Congressman Pace was unable to get Jimmy into the Naval Academy at that time. He suggested that Jimmy take more science classes and try again the following year. Jimmy followed the advice of one of his teachers and spent the year at Georgia Tech taking math and science courses and participating in the Reserve Officers' Training Corps (ROTC) program. He entered the U.S. Naval Academy in the summer of 1943.

Like most first year recruits, Jimmy spent his entire first year at Annapolis scared and homesick. The upperclassmen made fun of his

Southern hillbilly speech, and he was repeatedly whacked in the rear with serving spoons for failing to wipe the irrepressible smile off his face. He withstood a torrent of verbal abuse and more spanking for refusing to obey an upperclassman's order to sing "Marching through Georgia," the Civil War battle hymn of General Sherman's scorched-earth campaign across the state. Yet Jimmy was so absolutely determined to get through the year and go on, that he kept his feelings to himself. Years later he said, "It never entered my mind to quit – I mean not once."

Jimmy's best subjects were electronics, gunnery and naval tactics. He also took ballroom dancing and after-dinner speaking, and he ran cross-country. As part of the curriculum, he saw sea duty aboard the USS New York on East Coast-Caribbean patrol in 1944 – Carter's assignment was to clean the toilet troughs. He graduated fifty-ninth of eight hundred and twenty midshipmen in the accelerated class of 1946, and at that point he had made up his mind to be a career naval officer, hoping one day to be Chief of Naval Operations.

After graduating from Annapolis at age twenty-two, while still an ensign, Jimmy Carter married Rosalyn Smith. She was nineteen-years-old and had just graduated from high school as the valedictorian of her class.

While serving in the navy, Jimmy studied nuclear physics at Union College in Schenectady, New York, and was chosen to serve as an engineering officer aboard the Sea Wolf, an atomic submarine. Eight years later, and against his wife's wishes, Jimmy resigned from the navy to manage his family's farming interests when his father died. Carter became a millionaire as a peanut farmer.

During the next ten years Jimmy became a church deacon and chairman of the Sumper County Board of Education. In 1963 he was elected to the Georgia State Senate, and in 1970 he ran for governor and won. In 1976 Jimmy Carter ran as a dark horse candidate and won the Democratic nomination for president. He defeated President Gerald Ford in the election and became the thirty-ninth President of the United States.

After his term in office, former President Carter became involved in many humanitarian efforts and is well-known for his involvement with Habitat for Humanity. He also won the Nobel Peace Prize for brokering the peace treaty between Egypt and Israel.

More Information About Jimmy Carter	
State Represented	Georgia
Party Affiliation	Democrat
Siblings	First of Four Children
School(s) Attended	U.S. Naval Academy, Union College
Occupation(s)	Peanut Farmer, Naval Officer
Hobbies	Reading, Track/Cross Country, Basketball, Hiking, Bicycling, Bowling
Political Particulars In Office	Created Department of Education; Established national energy policy; Championed human rights; Brokered Camp David Accords (peace treaty between Egypt and Israel); Ratified Panama Canal Treaties; Established diplomatic relations with People's Republic of China; Negotiated SALT II treaty with Soviet Union; Iranian hostage crisis
States in Union During Teenage Years	Forty-eight

RONALD WILSON REAGAN

Fortieth President of the United States
Lived: 1911 – 2004   Served: 1981 – 1989

Ronald Reagan is the oldest president who has served in the White House to date. He was the only president who had been a professional actor, and he was the only president who had been divorced.

Ronald was born in his family's three-room rented apartment above a bakery on Main Street in Tampico, Illinois. It was a time when babies were usually born at home rather than in a hospital, and his mother hired a midwife to help her give birth. He was the younger of two sons. His father, John Reagan, was an alcoholic who lost and left jobs frequently. He would go for months at a time without taking a drink, and then he would disappear for a week or two, getting drunk while the family waited for his return. When he was sober, he traveled around looking for work, primarily as a shoe salesman, and he moved his family to a new town for a fresh start with each new job. By the time Ronald Reagan was nine, his family had moved five times. They finally settled in Dixon, Illinois, where he attended elementary and high school.

Ronald's mother Nelle was a warm-hearted, generous woman who regularly visited prisoners and tuberculosis patients. She took great care to make sure her children realized their father's alcoholism was a disease for which they should not resent him. During the Great Depression she supplemented the family's meager income by working as a salesclerk and seamstress at a local dress shop.

After dinner, the family regularly gathered in the living room and Nelle recited dramatic passages in impassioned tones. She organized local drama recitals, where young Reagan got his first taste of the theater. Ronald was chosen to perform in Sunday school plays, but he was shy and resented giving up his time outdoors to take part in rehearsals. Ronald's mother, with only an elementary school education, was determined her boys be well prepared for school, and she read extensively to them in their preschool years.

No one knew for twelve years that Ronald was extremely near-sighted – he assumed everyone saw the world as he did, with distant objects a mere blur. At school he made sure he sat in the front row, and because he had a photographic memory, he was able to cope with his undiagnosed handicap. Shortly before the discovery of his nearsightedness, Ronald discovered sports, football in particular. Once he thought about giving up the game, because of the violence in the sport, but his love of competition kept pulling him back. He remembered his mother's admonition not to give up and to keep trying at all costs… it was advice that would come back to him many times in his life.

Ronald was once nearly killed as he and his brother crawled under a steaming train just before it departed. In another incident he and a friend fired a hole in the ceiling of his house with an shotgun. When the Ringling Brothers Circus passed through Dixon, Reagan worked as an unskilled laborer, doing odd jobs for twenty-five cents an hour. In his spare time he collected bird eggs and butterflies, and raised pigeons and rabbits. Despite the poverty of his youth and the anguish of coping with his father's alcoholism, Reagan recalled his childhood as an extremely happy time in his life.

Reagan was taught to read by his mother when he was five-years-old. In grade school he usually earned A's in reading and math, and B's in other subjects. Ronald spent hours in the afternoon reading adventure books in the library.

He was active in many outdoor pursuits, but football was the center of his life. He practiced all summer for the fall football season, but as a freshman in high school he didn't even make the scrub team (those who didn't make first string). He was too small at five feet, three inches tall, and only one hundred and eight pounds. But Ronald didn't give up – he had his dream, and he was determined to make it come true. No matter how disappointed he felt sitting on the bench, he never missed a practice. Reagan shot up in his senior year to be six feet, one inch tall, and he gained thirty pounds, weighing in at one hundred and sixty five pounds. Ronald became a first-string football player, and a remarkable change came over him. He blossomed, was sociable and outgoing, and became one of the most popular kids in school.

Ronald also played basketball and did well on the track team. He was president of the student body and wrote for the yearbook. He joined the drama society and played the lead in Philip Barry's play, *You and I*. He found drama fun and exciting, and he finally understood why his mother loved to put on all the plays in Dixon.

Ronald wanted to go to college after graduating from high school, but he was going to have to pay his own way – his parents just didn't have the money to help put him through school. In the summer of 1926, at age fifteen, Ronald got a job at a local construction site digging foundations for thirty-five cents an hour. It was tough, boring labor, but it put muscles on his lean frame, and he earned two hundred dollars, which he put in the bank to use for his college education.

In 1927, at age sixteen, Ronald got a job as a lifeguard at Lowell Park that paid fifteen dollars a week. He started at eight in the morning and worked until sundown. He worked hard and learned a lot about people on the job. Over a period of seven summers, he rescued seventy-five people, and by the time he graduated from high school he had saved $400 to get him through the first year at Eureka College in Illinois.

During the Great Depression, Ronald was in college and low on funds. He got a job washing dishes at the Tau Kappa Epsilon fraternity in exchange for his room, and won a sports scholarship to pay for half of his tuition. In his junior and senior years, he paid his way working as the school's swim coach and pool lifeguard.

In college from 1928 – 1932, Reagan majored in economics and sociology, but spent most of his time away from the books. "I let football and other extracurricular activities eat into my study time," he admitted in a commencement address to Eureka graduates in 1982, "with the result that my grade average was closer to the C level required to maintain eligibility than it was to straight A's."

By the time he was ready to graduate in 1932, he was popular and well known on campus. His sports reputation was of a guy who never gave up. Like his mother, he had an optimist's knack for raising people's spirits and for taking the high road. An articulate young man with an opinion on everything, he was envied because he did well in school with very little studying. The night before an exam he'd thumb through the text for an hour and then, putting his photographic memory to good use, he would write a satisfactory paper the next day.

For three years Reagan was president of the Booster Club, a first-string guard on the football team, the principal basketball cheerleader, and the school's number one swimmer. As a member of the debate team, Ronald took an important part in college politics. He was also a feature editor for the yearbook, and for two years was a member of the student senate, serving one year as president.

Most significantly, Ronald was active in the drama society. In Edna St. Vincent Millay's *Aria da Capo*, Reagan played a shepherd who dies a moving, dramatic death. The drama society entered the play in the Eva Le Gallienne Competition at Northwestern University, going up against many drama departments, including those from Harvard and Yale. *Aria da Capo* took a coveted second place, and Ronald earned an honorable mention for his acting.

After graduating in 1932, Reagan decided to become a radio sports announcer. Finding a job during the Depression was difficult, but he hitchhiked from one city to another looking for work. Finally, the program director at WOC in Davenport, Iowa hired him. He did well in his job and moved to a larger station, WHO in Des Moines, Iowa. In 1937, when in California to cover spring training for the Chicago Cubs as a Headline radio announcer, Reagan took a screen test that led to a seven-year contract with the Warner Brother's studio. That was the beginning of a twenty-eight year career as an actor. He served six years as president of the Screen Actors Guild (SAG), a labor organization representing thousands of actors.

In 1940, at age twenty-nine, Ronald married the actress Jane Wyman, and eight years later they divorced. At age forty-one Reagan married again, this time to Nancy Davis. He had two children from each marriage, one of whom was adopted.

Originally a liberal Democrat, Reagan switched his allegiance to the Republican Party when Eisenhower ran for president. Prior to running for Governor of California, Reagan had no political experience other than his membership in many politically liberal organizations, which were later exposed as communist fronts. During Joseph McCarthy's witch-hunts of the early 1950's, Ronald became an FBI informant. After serving two terms as Governor of California, at sixty-nine-years-old, Ronald Reagan decided to run for president.

During his first term in office he survived an assassination attempt, and went on to serve two full terms as President of the United States.

More Information About Ronald Reagan	
Born	Illinois
State Represented	California
Party Affiliation	Republican
Siblings	Second of Two Children
Pet	Dog named "Rex"
School(s) Attended	Eureka College
Occupation(s)	Lifeguard, Swim Coach, Actor, Radio Announcer
Hobbies	Football, Basketball, Track, Swimming, Cheerleading, Acting, Debate
Political Particulars in Office	Nicknamed "The Great Communicator" by the media; Overhauled income tax code; Supply-side Economics; Anti-communism; Strategic Defense Initiative; Iran-Iraq War
States in Union During Teenage Years	Forty-eight

GEORGE HERBERT WALKER BUSH

Forty-First President of the United States
Lived: 1924 –   Served: 1989 – 1993

George Bush was the first vice-president since Martin Van Buren to be elected president at the end of his vice presidential term. Bush was the first president born in June, thus rounding out the year – presidents have been born in all twelve months of the year.

George was born in a makeshift delivery room in the family's Victorian home in Milton, Massachusetts. The second of five children, George has three brothers and a sister. Both his mother and father came from very wealthy families. His father, Prescott Bush, a graduate of Yale University, was a wealthy businessman who served as a U.S. Senator. His mother, Dorothy Walker Bush, was a remarkably versatile athlete, excelling in baseball, basketball, track and tennis. She was once runner-up for the girl's national tennis championship in Pennsylvania. A strict disciplinarian, she laid down house rules designed to prevent her children from being spoiled by the wealth around them, and to instill in them an aversion to boasting or self-promotion.

A biographer once wrote that George's father was "the greatest single influence" on his son's life. But George explained that this judgment was only partially correct. He said his mother's influence was just as important as his father's. His father taught him about duty and responsibility, and from his mother he learned the importance of relating to other people, of kindness and tenderness.

While George was still an infant, the family moved to Greenwich, Connecticut, which was considered an exclusive suburb of New York City. He was raised on Grove Lane, in the Deer Park section of Greenwich, in a nine bedroom Victorian-style home set on two acres of wooded property. Raised amid wealth and comfort, young George was driven to school, and out on early dates by the family chauffeur. The housekeeper, a Scottish nanny, maids, and a cook tended to the family's needs. The children were kept in line with spankings that were administered with a squash racket or similar instrument.

A versatile athlete and fierce competitor, George sometimes let his desire to win overtake good sportsmanship. While playing in a tennis tournament at age ten, he angrily ordered his aunt off the court for making too much noise. Some of George's fondest childhood memories are of summer vacations spent at his maternal grandfather's stone and shingle home on eleven acres at Walker's Point in Maine. There he combed the beach for starfish, learned to drive a motorboat, played tennis at the River Club, and fished for mackerel and pollack aboard his grandfather's boat, the *Tomboy*.

George attended the Greenwich Country Day School, where he played first base on the baseball team and was a running back on the football team. He also played soccer and tennis. An avid tennis player since the age of five, George developed his game in group lessons from Czech pro Karel Kozeluh. At age thirteen he enrolled at Phillips Academy, a very prestigious boy's prep school in Andover, Massachusetts. As a freshman, he underwent typical hazing rituals of that era, wearing a blue beanie and taking orders from seniors.

Most teachers remembered George as an unremarkable student who did little more than what was expected of him. A fellow Andover athlete who was in Bush's history and English classes said that out of the two hundred students in his class, maybe thirty could have become president, but George Herbert Bush wasn't one of them. He said George didn't seem to have the intellectual potential to become President of the United States, but he was well-liked by his teachers and fellow students, and he had many friends.

During his final year at Phillips, George became ill with a staph infection in his right arm, and he almost died. He spent many weeks in the Massachusetts General Hospital recovering. The slow recovery caused George to drop behind in his schoolwork by a year, but he still graduated by the age of eighteen because he had started grade school one year early.

Presidents Were Teenagers Too

In extracurricular activities, George was president of his senior class, captain of the baseball and soccer teams, manager of the basketball team, president of the Society of Inquiry that organized local charity drives, and editor of the school newspaper. He was voted second most influential with the faculty, third best athlete, third most popular, and third most handsome in his high school class.

Upon graduating from Phillips Academy in 1942, George ignored the advice of his counselor and the commencement speaker, Secretary of War Henry Stimson, who urged the graduates to go to college before joining the armed forces. On his eighteenth birthday George enlisted in the navy as a seaman second class. After undergoing extensive flight training, he earned his wings and a commission as an ensign, becoming the youngest pilot in the navy at that time. Toward the end of his training he was reprimanded for buzzing too near a local fairground, frightening a circus elephant, which broke from its handlers and fled into town. In another incident during a training exercise, the wheels on his plane collapsed, sending him into a belly landing on the tarmac. Although he was unhurt, his $96,000 aircraft was destroyed.

George was one of just four pilots in his original fourteen-pilot squadron to survive World War II. His most harrowing wartime experience was on a bombing mission against a Japanese radio center on the Bonin Islands. During his descent, the plane was struck by enemy anti-aircraft fire. Despite smoke filling the cockpit and flames eating away at the wings, George pressed toward the target, dropped his payload, and limped out to sea, where he yelled out the order to bail out and then bailed out himself. His tail-gunner was already dead from gunfire, and his radioman was killed in the fall.

Bush slammed into the tail of the aircraft during bailout, slicing open his scalp and tearing his parachute before splashing into the Pacific Ocean. He scrambled onto a yellow rubber raft and hand-paddled against the currents that were carrying him toward the Japanese boats. George remained in the water for more than three hours, nursing his head wound and a fresh sting from a man-of-war until he was rescued by an American submarine, the *Finback*. Had he been captured at sea by the Japanese boats, it is likely he would have fallen into the hands of Japanese authorities on the Bonin Islands who, after the war, were convicted of war crimes, including the torture, decapitation, and even cannibalization of downed American airmen. While in the navy, Bush flew fifty-eight combat missions, and he was awarded the Distinguished Flying Cross for his heroic and courageous service.

George served in the navy until September of 1945, rising to lieutenant. After returning home from the war he, at age twenty, married nineteen-year-old Barbara Pierce. Bush, then married with a child on the way, enrolled in Yale University's accelerated two-and-a-half year undergraduate program. He majored in economics and minored in sociology. He played first base on the Yale baseball team and was known as an outstanding fielder, but only a fair hitter who was often fooled by curve balls. He threw left-handed, batted right-handed, and in fifty-one games played during his two seasons on the team, kept a respectable .251 batting average. George played first base in the first College World Series in 1947.

Bush also played soccer on a team that won the New England collegiate championship. He joined and became president of the Delta Kappa Epsilon fraternity. As a senior, George, like William Howard Taft seventy years earlier, was inducted into Skull and Bones, Yale's venerable secret society. Bush's grades improved markedly in college – quite a turnaround from his mediocre academic performance in high school. He made the Phi Beta Kappa honor society, won the Francis Gordon Brown prize for all-around student leadership, and graduated with honors in the class of 1948.

Upon his graduation from Yale, Bush declined to join the investment firm with which his father had been associated, in order to strike out on his own. After reading Louis Bromfield's *The Farm*, he considered going into agriculture, but he could not afford the substantial initial investment required. He wound up working from the bottom up in the oil business, and started his own oil company with some financial help from his maternal uncle.

In 1967, at age forty-three, George Bush was elected to the U.S. House of Representatives. After his second term in Congress, he was chosen by Richard Nixon to serve as the U.S. Ambassador to the United Nations. Under President Ford, Bush was appointed to be the Director of the Central Intelligence Agency. In 1981 George Bush became vice president under President Ronald Reagan, and after two terms in that position, George Herbert Walker Bush was elected as the forty-first President of the United States.

More Information About George H.W. Bush

Born and Lived	b. Massachusetts, l. Connecticut
State Represented	Texas
Party Affiliation	Republican
Siblings	Second of Five Children
Pet	Dogs: English Springer Spaniels named *C. Fred* and *Millie*
School(s) Attended	Yale University
Occupation(s)	Navy Pilot, Businessman
Hobbies	Tennis, Fishing, Baseball, Football, Soccer
Political Particulars in Office	Tiananmen Square protests; Fall of the Berlin Wall; Invaded Panama to overthrow Manuel Noriega; Gulf War – U.N. invasion of Iraq in Operation Desert Storm; Soviet Union ceased to exist and the communist empire ended
States in Union During Teenage Years	Forty-eight

WILLIAM JEFFERSON CLINTON

Forty-Second President of the United States
Lived: 1946 –   Served 1993 – 2001

William Blythe IV never knew his father, William Blythe III, who was killed in an automobile accident at the age of twenty-nine, three months before his son was born. William Blythe III was a hard-working traveling salesman who sold heavy equipment. William's mother, Virginia Cassidy, was a twenty-year-old nursing trainee when William's father married her after a brief two-month courtship.

Four years after her husband's untimely death, Virginia married Roger Clinton, an automobile dealer. His abusive alcoholism led to their divorce in 1962, when William was sixteen-years-old. A few months after the divorce, and over William's objections, his mother remarried Roger. A short time later, when he was in high school, William Blythe IV legally changed his last name to Clinton, hoping to bring peace to a very troubled family. Four years later, in 1968, his stepfather died of cancer.

Bill was born in Hope, Arkansas. When he was not quite two-years-old, his maternal grandparents took him in temporarily, while his mother advanced her nurse's training in New Orleans. They ran a grocery store in a predominantly black part of town, and taught Bill how to count and read by age three. They impressed him at an early age with their racial tolerance amid the segregation that was then prevalent in Arkansas. From age four until age seven, he lived with his mother and stepfather in a small, single-story frame house in

Hope, and after age seven he grew up in modest circumstances in Hot Springs, Arkansas.

Bill Clinton had no full siblings. From his mother's second marriage he had a half-brother, Roger Clinton, Jr., who became a singer and television production assistant, and who later spent two years in prison for dealing drugs. Bill benefited from a close extended family of aunts, uncles and cousins.

His childhood was difficult because of his stepfather's alcoholism. On one occasion his stepfather flew into a drunken rage after hearing that his wife was going to visit a dying relative. He fired a gun in her direction, sending a bullet into the wall of their home. Mrs. Clinton called the police, and they locked him up for the night. When under the influence of alcohol, Bill's stepfather often hit Mrs. Clinton, leaving bruises, until the day that Bill, at fourteen-years-old, mustered the courage to confront him, warning him never to raise a hand to his mother again.

For a time the Clintons did not have indoor plumbing, presenting young Bill with a difficult dilemma at night, whether to resist nature's call until sunrise or brave a dark outhouse that had become a haven for snakes. Bill recalled in an interview one of his earliest memories of being mauled by a sheep: "When I was seven or eight, a ram butted me and cut my head open. I was too young, fat and slow to run, even after he knocked me down the second time. He must have butted me ten times. It was the awfullest beating I ever took and I had to go to the hospital for stitches."

At age five Bill attended Miss Mary Purkins' School for Little Folks in Hope, Arkansas. When the Clintons moved to Hot Springs, Bill was enrolled in the second grade at St. John's Catholic School, because his mother felt that he was not yet ready for a large public school. He excelled during his two years there, but once got a D in conduct for repeatedly shouting out answers without giving the others in his class a chance. Bill transferred to a public elementary school in fourth grade, and then went on to Central Junior High and Hot Springs High School. Bill was the kind of person who went up to everyone new in high school and said: "Hi. How are you? My name is Bill Clinton, and I'm running for something," whatever it was. Fellow students always thought that someday Bill would become president of something.

As a teenager, Bill worked part-time at a hospital and was active in the Masonic Youth Order of DeMolay, a civic organization for young people. Many local civic groups sought out Bill to chair their fund-raising drives and campaigns in the community. So many organizations recruited Bill that his high school principal had to put a stop to it – his activities were causing him to miss too much school.

In all other respects Clinton led a very typical childhood. He was a Boy Scout, sang in the church choir, played touch football and attended band camp every summer. Amid his busy schedule at school and his unpredictable home life, Bill found time and energy for music. He became a talented musician, playing tenor saxophone, making it into the all-state band, and winning first place in a state saxophone competition. Along with two other boys he formed a jazz trio that included a saxophone, piano and drums. The trio, which performed in sunglasses, was known as The Three Blind Mice.

An outstanding student, Bill earned his high school's Academically Talented Student Award, was a member of the Phi Beta Kappa National Honor Society and was a National Merit Scholarship semi-finalist. He was elected junior class president and served on the student council. Clinton graduated fourth of the 323 students in the class of 1964, at the age of eighteen.

Bill was already an avid reader of the daily newspaper, and he became increasingly interested in current events. When his family bought their first television set in 1955, Bill was fascinated with political news, especially the 1956 Democratic National Convention. He was the only person in his family who sat and watched it all on TV.

In 1963, when he was seventeen-years-old, Bill had a momentous year. He was moved to tears by Martin Luther King Jr.'s, *I Have a Dream* speech, and in July of that same year he traveled to Washington as one of Arkansas' "senators" in the American Legion Program, Boy's Nation. This program introduced the "senators" to the structure and functions of the federal government, while combining lectures and forums with visitations to federal agencies, institutions, memorials and historical spots in and around Washington, D.C. At an outdoor reception for the group at the White House, Bill shook hands with President John F. Kennedy, and the encounter had a profound effect on him. Using the occasion to criticize Republican foot-dragging on civil rights, Kennedy commended the assembled youth for adopting a resolution calling racial discrimination a "cancerous disease."

Although Clinton had considered becoming a doctor or a musician by the time he returned to Arkansas, he had decided on a career in politics. Bill chose to attend Georgetown University because of its excellent Foreign Service program and because it is in the nation's capital. He shared a stone cottage off campus with four other students, and the five boys had heated arguments about the Vietnam War, which Clinton opposed. Clinton was president of his freshman and sophomore classes in college, and during his junior year he worked part time in the office of Arkansas' junior senator.

In the wake of the riots after the assassination of the Reverend Martin Luther King, Jr. in April 1968, Clinton worked with the Red Cross to deliver food to the burned-out section of Washington. He relied on Red Cross decals applied to his white Buick to protect him from the anti-white wrath of the neighborhood. At the height of the Vietnam War in 1968, at age twenty-two, Clinton graduated with a degree in international affairs.

That October Bill sailed to England to begin study as a Rhodes Scholar at Oxford University. He was only the second student from Georgetown ever to win a Rhodes Scholarship, and it was the first time Bill didn't have to work while going to school. During his first year he shared a cottage with another American, a Palestinian, two white South Africans, and several Englishmen. Fascinated by his new surroundings, he spent his first two weeks at Oxford on all-day walking tours. He studied politics, philosophy and economics in his first year and focused more exclusively on politics, with emphasis on the Communist bloc, in his second year. One of his instructors recalled that Clinton was better in oral argument than on paper – his essay technique was not the best, but he was an avid reader and a skilled debater.

While at Oxford Bill took part in public demonstrations against American involvement in the Vietnam War, helping to organize a teach-in at the University of London. He also served as a Peace Marshall at a protest outside the American Embassy in London. He traveled whenever a break in his studies allowed – in December 1969 and January 1970 he traveled alone through Scandinavia, the Soviet Union and Czechoslovakia. In Prague he stayed for six days with a Czech family and got a firsthand view of the city less than two years after the Soviet Union had invaded to crush the reform government.

Instead of completing his third year of the Rhodes Scholarship, Bill returned to the United States in 1970 to accept a scholarship to Yale University Law School. To earn spending money he taught at a community college, worked for a Hartford city councilman and did investigative work for a lawyer in New Haven, Connecticut. Clinton received his law degree in 1973 at age twenty-six. As soon as he graduated from law school, he applied and was granted a teaching position at Yale Law School. He became one of the youngest law professors at the school, where he also met his wife Hillary Rodham. Clinton was elected Attorney General of Arkansas in 1976, and in 1978 he became the youngest Governor of Arkansas at age thirty-two.

After five terms as Governor, William Jefferson Clinton ran for the presidency at the age of forty-six, and became the forty-second President of the United States. He enjoyed unprecedented popularity throughout his two terms in office, despite his impeachment by the House of Representatives in 1998 and the scandal surrounding his relationship with a female White House intern.

More Information About William J. Clinton	
State Represented	Arkansas
Party Affiliation	Democrat
Siblings	First of Two Children
Pet	Dog: Chocolate Labrador Retriever named *Buddy*, and Cat named *Socks*
School(s) Attended	Georgetown University, Oxford University, Yale Law School
Occupation(s)	Lawyer, Professor
Hobbies	Saxophone
Political Particulars In Office	North American Free Trade Agreement; "Don't Ask, Don't Tell" policy about homosexuals serving in the military; Brady Bill for firearms waiting period; Personal Responsibility and Work Opportunity Act; Budget surplus; Peace-keeping forces in Bosnia; Bombed Iraq
States in Union During Teenage Years	Fifty

GEORGE WALKER BUSH

Forty-Third President of the United States
Lived: 1946 –   Served: 2001 – 2009

George Walker Bush was the second son of a president to assume the nation's highest office. The other was John Quincy Adams (1825–1829), the son of John Adams (1797–1801). George W. Bush became the first president since Benjamin Harrison in 1888 to win the presidency despite losing the nationwide popular vote.

Little George, as he was known as a child, was born in New Haven, Connecticut. Bush was a member of a distinguished political family, his paternal grandfather Prescott Bush served as a U.S. Senator from Connecticut (1952–1962), and his father George H.W. Bush served as the forty-first President of the United States (1989–1993).

George, the oldest of six children, spent his early years in Midland, Texas where he attended Sam Houston Elementary School. He was an extremely active and friendly child, and he was known as the class clown, always cracking jokes and wanting to be the center of attention – traits he carried with him throughout his life. He passed his days swimming, riding bikes and playing catcher on his Little League baseball team.

At age seven, George was deeply affected when his four-year-old sister Robin died of cancer. He was particularly upset because his parents never told him how ill she was – they were afraid he wouldn't be able to cope with her death. Young George had nightmares for a long time after her death.

While at San Jacinto Junior High School, George served as class president and was quarterback of the football team. When he was thirteen, his family moved to Houston, Texas, where he went to a private school. He became a class officer and played on the football team, until two years later, at age fifteen, when his parents decided to send him away to a private high school. George went to Phillips Academy, the same boarding school in Andover, Massachusetts, that his father attended. He was on his own for the first time, and his friends asked George what he had done wrong to be sent away to a boarding school. At that time, Texas boys who got shipped off to boarding school were usually in trouble with their parents, but in this case it was a family tradition.

George did not do well in the classroom. In fact, he did so badly he was afraid he might flunk out of school. The first essay he wrote in an English class was a complete failure – he misused big words he did not understand, and the teacher gave him a zero on his report. Although he never made the honor roll, George was popular on campus. He made friends easily, and earned the nickname "Lip" because he had an opinion about everything. He became the head cheerleader for the football team at the all boys' school, and he was a member of the rock-and-roll band "The Torqueys," even thought he didn't play an instrument – his job was to stand on stage and clap his hands. When he graduated from Phillips, he was popular enough to finish second in the vote for "Big Man on Campus."

George wanted to continue to follow in his father's footsteps by going to Yale University, but he didn't really have the grades to get in. He also applied to the University of Texas, but because George's father and grandfather had gone to Yale, he was admitted to the university to keep the legacy alive. Despite his own distinguished family history, as a student George was often annoyed by Yale's elite Ivy League atmosphere. He remained unassuming and unpretentious throughout his stay at Yale. He wore rumpled clothes and drove an old, beat up car. He also made little impact while at school – most of his professors didn't remember him being involved in campus activities. Instead, George focused his time on intramural sports and partying. As a freshman, he was a pitcher on the Yale baseball team, and he took up rugby two years later. He also belonged to Yale's infamous, elite, secret society Skull and Bones.

While at Yale, George developed a drinking problem. He joined the fraternity known to be the biggest-drinking, loudest-partying house on campus, geared mainly toward athletes. Many in this fraternity committed outlandish pranks and got in trouble with the authorities. Bush, who became president of the fraternity, just as his father had from the same fraternity, was often in the middle of the pranks. One night while walking home from a party where he had too much to drink, George suddenly lay down in the middle of the street and rolled himself home.

More than once Bush got in trouble with the law. During winter break one year, in what he described as "the infamous Christmas wreath caper," police arrested George and some friends for stealing a wreath from a department store. He was charged with disorderly conduct, but the charge was dropped after Bush and the others apologized for what they had done. Friends said that while George had a wild side, he never did anything bad enough to prevent him from becoming President of the United States. In fact, they said, most of the things that Bush got involved with could probably be blamed on a combination of immaturity and too much alcohol.

While college students across the country were marching for civil rights and against the Vietnam War, George was caught up in the controversy of his fraternity's practice of "branding" pledges. Bush and his fraternity brothers used a piece of heated metal to brand, or burn, the skin of prospective members. After this practice was exposed in the media, George defended the practice by saying that the branding was no worse than getting a cigarette burn.

George graduated from Yale University with a bachelor's degree in history in 1968, at age twenty-two, at the height of the Vietnam War. Both he and his father, a congressman at the time, were strong supporters of the war. Instead of volunteering for active duty, George W. decided to join the Texas Air National Guard. He scored the lowest acceptable grade on the pilot aptitude test, much lower than other, rejected candidates, and he neglected to fill out the part of the questionnaire that asked about illegal activity. Nevertheless, George was accepted into the Texas Air National Guard in 1968.

After finishing his training in 1970, at age twenty-four, George's life got wilder as he entered what he has called his irresponsible and nomadic years, when his life seemed to drift without direction. He rented a one-bedroom apartment and played full-day games of pool volleyball with other residents in one of the complex's six swimming pools. In 1971, at age twenty-five, George got his first full-time job selling agricultural products.

A short time later George visited his father for Christmas, and they got into a terrible argument over the younger George being drunk one night and causing pandemonium outside their home. At one point George W. challenged his father to go outside and fight man to man. The elder Bush was able to calm his son down, but the incident was troubling because by now he thought his son was old enough to be more mature. It was around the same time that George decided to return to school to get a graduate degree. He wanted to become a lawyer and applied to the University of Texas Law School, but his application was rejected. He then applied to Harvard Business School, one of the most prestigious business schools in the country. At twenty-seven years of age, George was admitted, and two years later he graduated with a master's degree in business administration (MBA).

George then returned home to Texas, and in 1976, at age thirty, while traveling with his family in Maine, was arrested for driving under the influence of alcohol. He pled guilty, paid a fine, and had his driver's license suspended for thirty days. After what he described as his period of irresponsible youth, George converted to a sober and religious lifestyle upon his fortieth birthday in 1986.

After losing an election for the House of Representatives at age thirty-one, George went into the oil drilling business. After a few mergers with other companies and some unsuccessful ventures, he decided to sell his stock and bail out. A few years later, in 1981, his father became Vice President of the United States under President Ronald Reagan. In 1988 George W. became a managing partner of the Texas Rangers baseball team, and in that same year his father was elected President of the United States.

George W. Bush waited another sixteen years before he ran again for public office. In 1994 he was elected Governor of Texas, and with his reelection in 1998, George became the first Texas Governor to win consecutive four-year terms. He was the first person ever to be elected a state governor whose father had been a U.S. President.

In the year 2000, George W. Bush ran for President of the United States. As the general election campaign neared its end, the gap in the polls between Bush and the Democratic candidate Al Gore narrowed to the closest of any election in forty years. On election day, the presidency hinged on the twenty-five electoral votes from Florida, where Bush led Gore by fewer than 1,000 popular votes after a mandatory statewide machine count. Concluding that a fair statewide recount could not be performed in time to meet the December 18 deadline for certifying the state's electors, the U.S. Supreme Court issued a controversial 5 to 4 decision to reverse the Florida Supreme

Court's recount order. Thus winning Florida, George Walker Bush narrowly won the electoral vote over former Vice President Gore by 271 to 266, only one more than the required 270.

More Information About George W. Bush	
Born	Connecticut
State Represented	Texas
Party Affiliation	Republican
Siblings	First of Six Children
Pet	Dogs: English Springer Spaniel named "Spot" and Scottish Terrier named "Barney"; Cat named "Willie"
School(s) Attended	Yale University, Harvard Business School
Occupation(s)	Oil businessman, Manager of baseball team
Hobbies	Baseball, Swimming, Football, Bicycling
Political Particulars in Office	Sept 11, 2001 terrorist attack by al-Queda; War against Taliban in Afghanistan; War in Iraq; Patriot Act; No Child Left Behind Act; Medicare Act
States in Union During Teenage Years	Fifty

BARACK HUSSEIN OBAMA

Forty-Fourth President of the United States
Lived: 1961 -   Served: 2009 -

Barack Obama, at age forty-seven, the junior U.S. Senator from Illinois, made history when he became the first African-American to be nominated by any major political party for the presidency of the United States of America at the Democratic National Convention on August 27, 2008.

His father, Barack Hussein Obama, Sr., was born and raised on a farm of the Luo tribe in Nyanza Province, Kenya, Africa. Barack's father was the first African exchange student at the University of Hawaii. Being a brilliant student in Kenya, he was selected to get a higher education so he could bring Western technology back to his third world country. He studied economics and graduated in three years at the top of his class. He received his Ph.D from Harvard University and returned to Kenya.

Barack Jr.'s mother, Ann Dunham, was born in Wichita, Kansas, and raised in various cities in the western United States before her father decided to settle down in Hawaii when Ann was in high school. After high school, she attended the University of Hawaii where she immersed herself in the studies of foreign cultures. Her love of reading would be passed along to her son and daughter.

In 1959, Ann, who was then an 18 year-old freshman, started dating Barack Sr., then 23, who she met in a Russian language class. After a brief courtship they eloped. In 1960, miscegenation, marriage between the races, was illegal in most states.

A year later, on August 4, 1961, Ann gave birth to Barack Hussein

Presidents Were Teenagers Too

Obama, Jr.

When Barack was two years old, his father won a scholarship to study at Harvard but did not have the money to take his family with him. He accepted the scholarship and never returned to the family, leaving Barack in Hawaii in his mother's care. Within a year they divorced.

Barack's mother, at age 26, remarried. She moved with her young son and new Indonesian husband, Lolo Soetoro, who was also a foreign student and graduate of the University of Hawaii, to his homeland in Indonesia, where Obama lived for four years. Soon after, they had a little girl, Maya.

Barack, who was six years old at the time, encountered new food, wild animals and an entirely foreign culture. He played in rice paddies and rode water buffalos. From his memoir he says, "I learned to eat small green chili peppers raw with dinner (with plenty of rice), and, away from the dinner table, I was introduced to dog meat (tough), snake meat (tougher), and roasted grasshopper (crunchy)."

It took Barack less than six months to learn the Indonesian language, its customs, and its legends. He survived chicken pox, measles, and the sting of his teacher's bamboo switches. He and his friends ran the streets morning and night hustling odd jobs, catching crickets, battling swift kites with razor-sharp lines – the loser watching his kite soar off with the wind.

While in Indonesia, Barack initially went to Fransiscus Asisi, a Catholic elementary school, with a registered name of Barry Soetoro. He then went to a government elementary school in Jakarta for two years. All classes were taught in the Indonesian language.

During the four years Barack lived in Indonesia, his mother insisted that he supplement his schooling by taking U.S. correspondence courses. So five days a week, she would roust her son out of bed before dawn, and teach him three hours of English before she went to her job at the American embassy instructing Indonesian businessmen in English.

While in Jakarta, his mother considered the lives of Indonesians and the lives of Americans –and she began thinking about how many more opportunities would be available to her son in the United States, where she thought Barack could receive a superior education. Although he attended Muslim and Catholic schools in Indonesia, his advancement was not up to the standards that his mother desired.

Barack was raised as much by his maternal grandparents, as his mother, who was traveling the globe studying other cultures. Both his mother and grandparents played a vital role in shaping the crux of his character. "Everything that is good about me, I got from my mother," he once said.

After living in Indonesia for four years, Barack and his half-sister, Maya, were sent back to Hawaii without his mother or step-father to live with his grandparents. Once there he was enrolled in the very prestigious college preparatory Punahou School in Honolulu which took students from kindergarten through 12th grade. The school was 90% white with a smattering of Asians. His grandparents had sacrificed their own prosperity for the sake of Obama and his sister.

In 1971, at the age of ten, he was introduced to his classroom on the first day of school by a kindly teacher, Miss Hefty, who heard giggles when she used his full name.

"Barack is such a beautiful name," said Miss Hefty, who had lived in Kenya herself and had been delighted to learn that the new boy's father was Kenyan. "It's such a magnificent country. Do you know what tribe your father is from?"

"The Luo tribe," Obama replied. When a student hooted like a monkey, the whole class laughed. Before the day was over, a red-haired girl asked if she could touch his hair, and another boy asked if his father was a cannibal?

Barack loved to play soccer, badminton, and chess, games he learned from his Indonesian step-father while living in Jakarta. Although a friendly kid, Barack spent most of his time reading comic books, watching TV, and listening to the radio.

Also at age ten, Obama received a visit from his father who he had not seen for the prior eight years. He learned that his father had remarried and that he now had five half-brothers and another half-sister who lived in Kenya.

All he remembers from his father's visit was how his father screamed at his mother and grandmother for letting Barack watch too much TV. The father believed that his son had been studying too little.

Barack was beginning to feel the pain of a failed marriage, his father's abandonment, and his mixed racial heritage. Suddenly Barack realized that his father somehow leapfrogged from being a goat herder in a poor, small isolated village in Africa to getting a scholarship to the University of Hawaii to going to Harvard and getting his Ph.D. This was the last time Barack saw his father. At the age of twenty-one, he received a phone call from one of his step-brothers in Kenya that his father, just forty-four years old, died in an automobile accident.

At this time in his life, Barack lived in a two-bedroom apartment in Honolulu, with his grandparents. Fortunately, his schoolmates were from well off families and weren't overtly cruel. Even though he was a rare African-American at this school, they didn't beat him up or call him names. When it came to prejudice and discrimination, growing up in Hawaii was quite different from growing up in the rest of the United States.

He says of himself in his memoir, "When I was in the 7th grade, I was such a terror in school that the teacher didn't know what to do with me."

When Obama was thirteen, his mother pleaded with him to come with her and Maya to Indonesia where she planned to do the field-work necessary for her degree. He refused. He liked his school and his friends so much he didn't want to leave.

Barack's days were filled with normal adolescent activities of a teenager in the mid-1970's seeking to understand what attracts the opposite sex, attending parties in which alcohol and marijuana were the main courses, hanging out at the beach, bodysurfing, and playing sports.

By the time Barack reached high school, his mother had separated from her second husband.

Although Barack played defensive lineman on the freshman foot-ball team, which he didn't really care for, he loved to play basketball. It was the first time he found something he had a passion for. Obama practiced many hours a day alone on a playground near his apartment. He was good enough to make the high school team. It was on the basketball court that he found a community of friends, white and black. It was here that he made his closest white friends, and where being black wasn't a disadvantage.

In was the books he read while he was in high school that solidi-fied his identity. He read many books by well known black writers: James Baldwin, Ralph Ellison, and Richard Wright. It was also at this time he was beginning to take an interest in writing. He was on the staff of his high school's literary journal, *The Living Water.* Other than that he was not an outstanding student. By his own account he received only "marginal grades." For Barack Obama, reading for information and for pleasure, became more important than grades.

To most of Obama's white friends at school, he was just a normal guy who didn't seem to have black white issues. If they were there, he kept them concealed quite well. There was little racial tension at the school.

Barack had something in common with many African-American males, he lacked a father in his life to council him through these confusing times. For a while he fell into the exaggerated stereotypes of black male behavior. He stopped focusing on his studies, and instead played a lot of sports, seeking respectability. He grew a thick Afro and donned a stylish open-collared leisure suit with fat lapels, making himself stand out in the crowd in an urban black way. Obama cherished his full Afro and spent an undue amount of time picking it to make it appear just right.

Barack was always a B student, but by his senior year, he was slacking off in his schoolwork in favor of basketball, beach time and parties. He also dabbled in drugs and alcohol. He would buy a six-pack of beer after school and drink them while shooting baskets.

His grandparents became concerned about his declining grades, his possible drug use and overall lack of direction. Because he was black, they were afraid he would be used as a courier to supply his white friends with drugs. As a supplier this could lead him into big time trouble with the law.

His homeroom teacher, Eric Kusunoki, said Barack was a good student but one who had failed to reach his potential. Although he would eventually go to Harvard, he never stood out academically in high school, mostly from lack of effort. "All of the teachers acknowledged that he was a sharp kid," Kusunoki said, "Sometimes he didn't challenge himself enough or he could have done better."

In 1979, at age eighteen, after being accepted by several colleges, Barack chose to attend Occidental College on a full scholarship. He decided on this college because he was fond of a particular girl attending there whom he had met in Hawaii while she was vacationing. His academic goals at that time were not all that clear.

Occidental was a powerful intellectual growth experience for Obama even if he did not perform well in his studies. But it was here that he slowly drifted away from his great interest in basketball. Instead of partying, he found deep-thinking peers and professors, who challenged him to see the world in global terms. Instead of the basketball courts, he found himself in coffeehouses discussing the highly intellectual concerns of the day.

After his sophomore year at Occidental, in 1981, at the age of twenty, Obama transferred to Columbia University in New York City. Here he chose to live a monastic existence spending time alone and digesting the works of some of the great thinkers of the past. "I had tons of books. I read everything. I think that was the period when I grew as much as I have ever grown intellectually," Obama said in his memoir.

He spent the next two years at Columbia. He lived in a run down apartment building in East Harlem, while working for a construction company. It was here at Columbia that Obama started studying in earnest. Instead of going to bars, he started running three miles every day, fasted on Sundays, and began keeping a journal. When his mother and Maya visited in the summer of 1982, they found a young man far different from the disaffected slacker they would have encountered had they dropped by his dorm at Occidental three years before. Obama graduated Columbia University in 1983, at the age of twenty-two, with a Bachelor of Art's degree in political science.

After graduating from Columbia, Barack decided he wanted to be a community organizer in south Chicago to help the poor people there.

After three frustrating years as a community organizer, Barack applied and got into Harvard Law School at the age of twenty-seven. After four years he graduated magna cum laude. While there he became the first African-American to become the president of the prestigious Harvard Law Review. It was Lawrence Tribe, a distinguished law professor from Harvard, who said, "Obama is one of the two most talented students I've had in thirty-seven years. He's a guy I hope will be president one day. "

While every door was open to him to get a high paying job, he chose to go to work for a low paying law firm which specialized in Civil Rights cases. He also found time to teach constitutional law at the University of Chicago Law School.

Obama's advocacy work led him to run for the Illinois State Senate as a Democrat. He was elected in 1996 at the age of thirty-five. After an unsuccessful run for the United States House of Representatives, he decided to run for the United States Senate in 2004 and won garnering 70% of the votes.

In 1992, Barack married Michelle Robinson, a Princeton and Harvard graduate, and also a practicing attorney.

Barack was thirty-three when his mother died of ovarian cancer at the age of fifty-three. A year later he published his first memoir, *DREAMS OF MY FATHER: A Story of Race and Inheritance,* in 1995 at the age of thirty-four. His second book, *THE AUDACITY OF HOPE: Thoughts on Reclaiming the American Dream,* was published in 2006.

On November 4, 2008, Democratic candidate, U.S. Senator Barack Obama, beat the Republican candidate, U.S. Senator John McCain, with an electoral vote of 364 to 174 to become the 44th president of the United States of America.

More Information About Barack Obama	
Born	Hawaii
State Represented	Illinois
Party Affiliation	Democrat
Siblings	First of seven children: five half-brothers; and two half-sisters
School(s) Attended	Occidental, Columbia, Harvard Law School
Occupation(s)	Community Organizer, Attorney
Hobbies	Basketball, Badminton, Chess
States in Union During Teenage Years	Fifty

DONALD JOHN TRUMP

Forty-fifth President of the United States

Lived: 1946 -   Served: 2017 -

Trump was born on June 14, 1946, in Jamaica Estates, Queens, a neighborhood in New York City. He was the second youngest child of five children. Trump's older brother Fred Jr. died in 1981 from alcoholism, which Trump says led him to avoid trying alcohol or cigarettes.

Trump is of German ancestry on his father's side and Scottish ancestry on his mother's side; all four of his grandparents were born in Europe. His father Fred Trump was born in Queens to parents from Kallstadt, Germany and became one of the biggest real estate developers in New York City. His mother, Mary Trump (née MacLeod) was born in Tong, Lewis, Scotland. Fred and Mary met in New York and married in 1936, settling together in Queens.

When Donald was 12 years old in 1958, he and his boyhood friend, Peter, were always hungry for adventure. Unbeknownst to his parents, they would board a train bound for Manhattan where all the action was. They were fascinated by Times Square where they could buy stink bombs, hand buzzers and fake vomit —perfect accessories for playing pranks on their pals back at school. Manhattan would be their testing grounds.

The Trumps had things hardly anyone else possessed, including a chauffeur, a cook, an intercom system, a color television, and a sprawling electric train set that was the envy of the neighborhood.

While other kids rode their Schwinn bicycles, Donald would cruise by on a ten-speed Italian racer.

At times Donald's fearlessness impressed one of his babysitters, Frank Briggs. One evening Briggs took Donald into a sewer that was under construction. They remained underground for two hours. "All of a sudden it was pitch black and you couldn't see the entrance," Briggs recalled. "And the thing that amazed me was that Donald wasn't scared. He just kept walking."

When Donald was ready for kindergarten, the Trumps sent him to the private Kew-Forest School, where they had enrolled his older brother, Fred Jr.

At Kew-Forest, Donald encountered a dress code –ties and jackets for boys and skirts for girls – and a strict set of rules, including the requirement that students rise at their desks when a teacher entered the classroom. From the start, Donald and his friends resisted their teachers' commands, disrupting class with wisecracks and unruly behavior. *"We threw spitballs and we played racing chairs with our desks, crashing them into other desks,"* recalled a fellow student. Donald spent so much time in detention that his friends nicknamed the punishment the DT's –short for *"Donny Trumps."*

In second grade, after Donald yanked a girl's pigtails, she raised her metal lunchbox and brought it down on Donald's head. No matter the consequences, Donald's behavior did not change. *"He was headstrong and determined,"* said one of his teachers. *"In the cafeteria, he would sit with his hands folded, with this look on his face –I use the word surly – almost daring you to say one thing or another that wouldn't settle with him."*

One day a neighbor of Donald's said his own impression of Donald was cemented in his brain when he saw Donald jump off his bike and pummel another boy. "It was so unusual and terrifying to see that happen at that age," he said.

Trump's primary focus in elementary school was *"creating mischief because, for some reason, I liked to stir things up and I liked to test people. It wasn't malicious so much as it was aggressive."*

As a second grader, as Trump has described it, he punched his music teacher, giving him a black eye. I didn't think he knew anything about music, and I almost got expelled. I'm not proud of that, but it was clear evidence that even early on I had a tendency to stand up and make my opinion known in a very forceful way."

Trump's grades suffered and his behavior got him in hot water. He found success in his gym classes and playing sports, where his athletic prowess was unmistakable. He was number one in dodgeball as well as in baseball. In dodgeball he was the last man standing. By sixth grade, Donald's ability as a right-handed hitter was fearsome enough that opponents shifted toward left field to defend against him. *"If he had hit the ball to right field, he could have had a home run, because there was no one there. But, he always wanted to hit the ball through people. He wanted to overpower them."*

For all his wealth, Donald's father didn't want to spoil his children. He encouraged them to earn money by collecting empty White Rock soda bottles and turning them in for the nickel deposit. Donald also delivered newspapers.

Trump's parents ran a disciplined household forbidding their children to call each other by nicknames, wear lipstick, or go to bed past their curfew. The Trumps questioned their children each night about their homework and demanded that they perform their chores. Even so, Donald rebelled against the rules, arguing with his father. His father always told Donald that he was "KING," and that he needed to become a "killer" in anything he did.

While all this discipline was going on at home, Donald and his friend Peter created a routine that they kept secret from their parents. On Saturday mornings they would go to Times Square. They were drawn to the selection of switchblades. Because they liked *Westside Story* so much they envisioned themselves as gang members. They would end up buying these six-inch switchblades and play the game of *"LAND,"* in which they flung their knives at the ground and then stepped on the spot where the blade had pierced the dirt. Eventually, as they became more daring, they would graduate to buying and using 12 inch switchblades.

After his father found the switchblades in his son's bedroom, he decided it was time to send Donald to military school where he stayed for the next five years. He was 13 when he entered the New York Military Academy. The school was located in tiny Cornwall-on-Hudson, on a campus with a culture so strict and unforgiving that that one desperate cadet jumped into the Hudson River to swim to freedom.

Instead of adhering to his father's commands, Donald had a new master, a gruff, barrel-chested combat soldier named Theodore Dobias. Two afternoons a week Dobias would set up a boxing ring and order cadets with poor grades and those who had disciplinary problems to fight each other, whether they wanted to or not. "He *could be a fucking prick,"* Trump said. *"He absolutely would rough you up. You had to learn to survive."* The idea was to inject discipline and direction into boys who arrived on campus unformed and untamed.

Donald's competitive drive took over as he learned to master the academy. He won medals for neatness and order. He loved competing to win contests for cleanest room, shiniest shoes, and best-made bed. For the first time, he took pride in his grades; he grew angry when a study partner scored higher on a chemistry test. *"I finessed him (the teacher),"* Trump would say. *"It helped that I was a good athlete, since he was the baseball coach and I was the captain of the team. But I also learned to play him."*

To fellow cadets, Donald could be friendly or aloof or cocky. One day he would tell his fellow cadet, *"I'm going to be famous one day."*

As a senior, Donald drew notice for bringing women to campus and showing them around. "They were beautiful, gorgeous woman dressed in Saks Fifth Avenue," said his classmate. Trump was never shy about judging a girl's appearance, pronouncing one of the visitors a "dog." Donald Trump was identified as a "ladies man" in his senior yearbook.

While at the Academy, Donald would do anything to win. He just wanted to be first in everything, and he wanted people to know he was first. Off the field, Trump rose steadily from private to corporal to, in his junior year, supply sergeant, and finally to captain. It was said that you could always go to Donald and he would figure out how to get things done. As captain, Trump was said to be "even-keeled," inspiring respect. He didn't scream at his cadets. *"You just didn't want to disappoint him,"* said one of his fellow cadets.

After graduating from the military academy, Trump attended Fordham University in the Bronx for two years, beginning in

August 1964. He then transferred to the prestigious Wharton School of Finance and Commerce at the University of Pennsylvania, which offered one of the few real estate studies departments in United States academia. While there, he worked at the family's company, Elizabeth Trump & Son, named for his paternal grandmother. Trump graduated from Wharton in May 1968 with a Bachelor of Science in Economics.

In 1971 he took control of his family's real estate and construction firm, Elizabeth Trump & Son, and renamed it The Trump Organization. He later expanded the business with other products and activities. Trump has built office towers, hotels, casinos, golf courses, and other Trump-branded facilities worldwide. He owned the Miss USA pageants from 1996 to 2015. From 2004 to 2015, Trump hosted and co-produced *The Apprentice*, a reality television series on NBC

After a contentious primary election, with 16 other presidential candidates, Donald Trump, one of two candidates, who never before held public office, won. He went on to become the presidential nominee for the Republican Party in the general election. Against very strong odds, he won the presidential election against Hilary Clinton to become the 45th president of the United States. Although he won the Electoral College vote 290 to 232, he lost the popular vote by more then two million votes. At 70 years old, he will be the oldest person ever to assume the presidency of the United States.

More Information About Donald Trump	
Born	New York
State Represented	Never Held Public Office
Party Affiliation	Republican
Siblings	Two sisters and two brothers
School(s) Attended	Fordham and Wharton at U of Pennsylvania
Occupation(s)	Real Estate Developer and TV Entertainer
Hobbies	Golf
States in Union During Teenage Years	Fifty

AFTERWORD

I had only one objective for writing this book – to inspire teenagers to follow their dreams and strive to reach their inherent potential as human beings. I wanted to show that no matter what one's background may be, anything is possible, including becoming President of the United States.

It didn't take long into my research to realize that there were all kinds of twists and turns during the formative years of this nation's first forty-three presidents. By the time I finished writing, the "early" years had grown to include the mid-twenties and even some mid-thirties. I found it amazing where these men had been, and how they ended up becoming Presidents of the United States of America.

A major factor for success is a strong desire to win. It is not surprising then, to find so many presidents involved in athletics and debate when they were teenagers. If we look at the professions they chose, we find that twenty-five of forty-three presidents were lawyers. Many were leaders in the military and some were independent businessmen. If we never confront obstacles and adversity in our lives, we will never have the opportunity to build the armor we need to be fighters, to learn determination and perseverance.

In many cases the early years of former presidents were average and uneventful. Many were not outstanding students as teenagers, and many did not come from wealthy families. Some were not particularly ambitious or aggressive, while others were even weak, frail and sickly.

It is my feeling that there are characteristics that allow some men (and soon women) to attain the highest office in the United States. Can it be true that some people come into the world with built-in self-esteem and self-confidence that allow them to take on leadership roles? That no matter how many times they fail, they keep coming back, while others fail once and never try again? It is this ability to rebound that I believe is significant in all these leaders' lives.

The history of our previous presidents is proof that the opportunity exists for almost anyone, regardless of his position or status, to become president. There are no physical requirements. James Madison was only five feet, four inches tall, and weighed a lean one hundred pounds. William Howard Taft weighed in at a hefty three hundred and thirty two pounds – a special bathtub had to be built for him in the White House. Statistically the average president, to date, was five feet, ten inches tall, and weighed one hundred and eighty pounds.

There are also no educational requirements for the job of president. No college degree or special training is required, and while most presidents graduated from college, six never attended and three dropped out. Some presidents did extremely well in school, while others were poor or mediocre students. There were a few who never had any formal education at all, including Abraham Lincoln. Our seventeenth president, Andrew Johnson, barely knew how to read and write by the time he was sixteen-years-old.

Not all Presidents had a mother and a father when they needed them the most. Three presidents were born after their fathers had died (Jackson, Hayes, Clinton). Six lost their fathers before they were twelve-years-old (Washington, Jefferson, A. Johnson, Lincoln, Garfield, Hoover). Three presidents lost their mothers before they were fourteen (Jackson, Tyler, Coolidge), and two were adopted (Ford and Clinton).

Parents and teachers can provide children with a solid foundation and give them the tools to succeed, but individuals must possess self-motivation, self-worth and self-confidence. Life can be challenging, and no one goes through life without some obstacles.

Striving to achieve was found to be the most important attribute shared by the men who have become United States Presidents.

Presidents of the United States have come from all walks of life, from many different states in the nation, were born in various positions in their families, and have a variety of temperaments and personality types. It is remarkable how dissimilar the backgrounds of all our presidents are. Although it is truly impossible to predict anyone's future, there are far more doors open today than ever before. This is why I say, *"You too could be President of the United States of America."*

Family Order of U.S. Presidents

Only child	3
Oldest child	13
Second child	14
Third child	5
Fourth child	0
Fifth child	2
Sixth child	2
Seventh child	1
Youngest child	2

Consulting with more than one hundred historians, a group of psychologists came up with the following categories to see what personal, psychological traits each President had:

Psychological Traits

Introverts	J. Adams, J.Q. Adams, Nixon, Hoover, Coolidge, Buchanan, Wilson, B. Harrison
Extroverts	F.D. Roosevelt, Kennedy, Clinton, T. Roosevelt, Reagan, W.H. Harrison, Harding, Jackson, L.B. Johnson
Good Guys	Hayes, Taylor, Eisenhower, Tyler, Fillmore, Cleveland, Ford, Washington
Actors	Reagan, Harding, B. Harrison, Clinton, Pierce
Dominators	L.B. Johnson, Nixon, A. Johnson, Jackson, Polk, T. Roosevelt, Arthur
Innocents	Taft, Harding, Grant
Maintainers	McKinley, G.H.W. Bush, Truman
Philosophers	Garfield, Lincoln, Jefferson, Madison, Carter, Hayes
Unable to categorize	Van Buren and Monroe

References Used As Source Material

World Book Encyclopedia – 1965

The Lives of Our Presidents – Jesse Lyman Hurlbut - The John C Winston Co. 1925

The Complete Book of U.S. Presidents - William A Degregorio - Wing Books 1993

The American Presidents - David Whitney - Doubleday & Co. 1967

Presidential Anecdotes - Paul F. Boller Jr. - Oxford University Press - 1981

The Mothers of American Presidents - Doris Faber – The New American Library - 1968

A Child's Life of George Washington - Louise Embree - E.P Dutton - 1932

George Washington - Lucile Falkof - Garett Educational Corp. (G.E.C.)- 1989

John Adams - The American Heritage Book of Presidents - 1967

Thomas Jefferson - Marvin Barrett - Random House - 1967

The World of Young Tom Jefferson - Suzanne Hilton - Walker and Co. - 1986

Young Tom Jefferson - Francis Sabin - Troll Associates - 1986

James Madison - Barbara G. Polikoff - G.E.C. -

James Monroe - Christine Maloney Fitz-Gerald – Encyclopedia. of Presidents - 1987

James Monroe Young Patriot - Rae Bains - Troll Associates - 1986

Andrew Jackson - William Gutman - Barrons Educational Press - 1987

Zachary Taylor - David R. Collins - G.E.C. -

Ulysses S. Grant - Lucille Falkof- G.E.C. -

Ulysses S. Grant: A Biography - William S. McFeely

Rutherford B. Hayes - Neil Robbins - G.E.C. - 1989

The Life of James Garfield: Teacher, Soldier, President - Bill Severn - 1964

Grover Cleveland - David R. Collins - G.E.C.- 1988

Benjamin Harrison - Elizabeth P Meyers - Reielly and Lee Books - 1969

Benjamin Harrison - Reta Stevens - G.E.C. -

Theodore Roosevelt - Rebecca Stefoff - G.E.C.

Theodore Roosevelt: The Strenuous Life - John A. Garraty - American Heritage - 1967

Woodrow Wilson - David Collins - G.E.C. - 1989

The Preparation of Calvin Coolidge -Robert A. Woods -Houghton Mifflin Co. 1924

On Herbert Hoover Growing Up - William Nichols - William Morrow and Co. - 1962

Franklin D. Roosevelt - John Devaney - Walker and Co.

Presidents Were Teenagers Too

Harry S. Truman: Plain Speaking - Merle Miller - A Berkeley Medallion Book - 1974

Harry S. Truman - David Collins - G.E.C.

IKE: His Life and Times - Piers Brendon - Harper and Row - 1986

Young John Kennedy - Gene Schoor -McFadden Bartell Books - 1963

JFK: Boyhood to Whitehouse - Bruce Lee - Fawcett Publications - 1961

Lyndon Bains Johnson: Young Texan - Thomas Frank Barton - Bobbs-Merrill -1973

Richard Nixon: The Education of a Politician - Stephen E. Ambrose - Memoirs of Richard Nixon

Jimmy Carter - Betty Covington Smith - Walker and Co. 1986

James E. Carter - Daniel Richman - G.E.C.- 1989

Ronald Reagan - Where Is The Rest of Me?

George Bush –William Pemberton –Rourke Publications, Inc –1993

Bill Clinton – Michael D. Cole – Enslow Publishers – 1994

George W. Bush–Heron Marquez –Lerner Publications Co. –2002

Dreams from My Father – Barack Obama- Three River Press - 2004

Obama: From Promise to Power – David Mendell – Harper Collins - 2007

Hopes and Dreams: The Story of Barack Obama – Steve Dougherty – 2008

APPENDIX A

POPULATION OF THE UNITED STATES — 1790 to 1960
America's population has risen steadily since the first census. The greatest percentage growth took place in the early years, with increases of more than a third in a ten-year period. The largest total increase took place between 1950 and 1960, when almost 28,000,000 persons were added to the population.

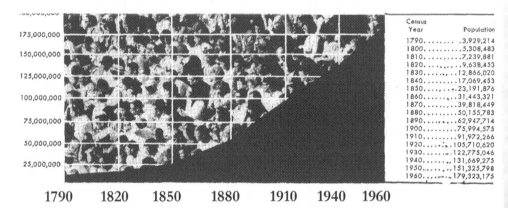

Census Year	Population
1790	3,929,214
1800	5,308,483
1810	7,239,881
1820	9,638,453
1830	12,866,020
1840	17,069,453
1850	23,191,876
1860	31,443,321
1870	39,818,449
1880	50,155,783
1890	62,947,714
1900	75,994,575
1910	91,972,266
1920	105,710,620
1930	122,775,046
1940	131,669,275
1950	151,325,798
1960	179,323,175

INDEX

Index

Index

Index

About The Author

Benny Wasserman was born and raised in Detroit, Michigan. After spending two years in the U.S. Army he attended a technical trade school in Los Angeles. He spent the next 34 years in the Aerospace Industry as an electronic engineer working on communication space satellites. He has been married for 58 years to his wife Fernie. They have three sons, two of whom are attorneys, and one is a physician. Because of hardships he endured as a youth, he has had a lifelong interest in the welfare of children. You can contact the author at <u>wass ben@aol.com</u>

Printed in the United States
By Bookmasters